MASTERS' BADGES
of the
City of London
Livery Companies

The Lord Mayor's Jewel

This pendant, dating from 1799, consists of a Sardonyx Cameo set in gold and enclosed in a Garter of gold and dark blue enamel bordered with rose-cut diamonds.

MASTERS' BADGES

of the
City of London
Livery Companies

RICHARD GODDARD

PHILLIMORE

Published 2011

Published by
PHILLIMORE & CO. LTD
Andover, Hampshire, England

www.phillimore.co.uk

© Richard Goddard, 2011

ISBN 978-1-86077-727-1

Printed and bound in Great Britain

Contents

Acknowledgements viii
Introduction ix
Foreword by the Rt. Hon. The Lord Mayor xi
Illustration Acknowledgements xii
List of Subscribers xiii

Part I

  I   How it all began 1
 II   Silversmiths and Designers 9
III   Lost, Stolen or Strayed. 17
IV   The Influence of Heraldry 20

Part II

The Worshipful Company of Mercers 27
The Worshipful Company of Grocers 29
The Worshipful Company of Drapers 31
The Worshipful Company of Fishmongers.. 33
The Worshipful Company of Goldsmiths 35
The Worshipful Company of Merchant Taylors 37
The Worshipful Company of Skinners.. 39
The Worshipful Company of Haberdashers 41
The Worshipful Company of Salters 43
The Worshipful Company of Ironmongers 45
The Worshipful Company of Vintners.. 47
The Worshipful Company of Clothworkers 49
The Worshipful Company of Dyers 51
The Worshipful Company of Brewers 53
The Worshipful Company of Leathersellers 55

The Worshipful Company of Pewterers. 57
The Worshipful Company of Barbers. 59
The Worshipful Company of Cutlers. 61
The Worshipful Company of Bakers.. 63
The Worshipful Company of Wax Chandlers. 65
The Worshipful Company of Tallow Chandlers 67
The Worshipful Company of Armourers and Brasiers 69
The Worshipful Company of Girdlers 71
The Worshipful Company of Butchers.. 73
The Worshipful Company of Saddlers 75
The Worshipful Company of Carpenters 77
The Worshipful Company of Cordwainers 79
The Worshipful Company of Painter-Stainers 81
The Worshipful Company of Curriers 83
The Worshipful Company of Masons 85
The Worshipful Company of Plumbers. 87
The Worshipful Company of Innholders 89
The Worshipful Company of Founders. 91
The Worshipful Company of Poulters 93
The Worshipful Company of Cooks 95
The Worshipful Company of Coopers 97
The Worshipful Company of Tylers and Bricklayers 99
The Worshipful Company of Bowyers 101
The Worshipful Company of Fletchers 103
The Worshipful Company of Blacksmiths 105
The Worshipful Company of Joiners and Ceilers 107
The Worshipful Company of Weavers 109
The Worshipful Company of Woolmen 111
The Worshipful Company of Scriveners 113
The Worshipful Company of Fruiterers 115
The Worshipful Company of Plaisterers 117
The Worshipful Company of Stationers and Newspaper Makers.. 119
The Worshipful Company of Broderers 121
The Worshipful Company of Upholders 123
The Worshipful Company of Musicians 125
The Worshipful Company of Turners 127
The Worshipful Company of Basketmakers 129
The Worshipful Company of Glaziers and Painters of Glass 131
The Worshipful Company of Horners 133
The Worshipful Company of Farriers. 135
The Worshipful Company of Paviors 137
The Worshipful Company of Loriners 139
The Worshipful Society of Apothecaries 141
The Worshipful Company of Shipwrights 143
The Worshipful Company of Spectacle Makers. 145
The Worshipful Company of Clockmakers. 147
The Worshipful Company of Glovers 149
The Worshipful Company of Feltmakers 151
The Worshipful Company of Framework Knitters 153
The Worshipful Company of Needlemakers 155

The Worshipful Company of Gardeners 157
The Worshipful Company of Tin Plate Workers 159
The Worshipful Company of Wheelwrights 161
The Worshipful Company of Distillers . .. .163
The Worshipful Company of Pattenmakers 165
The Worshipful Company of Glass Sellers 167
The Worshipful Company of Coachmakers & Coach Harness Makers 169
The Worshipful Company of Gunmakers 171
The Worshipful Company of Gold and Silver Wyre Drawers. 173
The Worshipful Company of Makers of Playing Cards . .. .175
The Worshipful Company of Fan Makers 177
The Worshipful Company of Carmen 179
The Honourable Company of Master Mariners 181
The Worshipful Company of Solicitors of the City of London.. 183
The Worshipful Company of Farmers 185
The Guild of Air Pilots and Air Navigators . .. .187
The Worshipful Company of Tobacco Pipe Makers 189
The Worshipful Company of Furniture Makers 191
The Worshipful Company of Scientific Instrument Makers 193
The Worshipful Company of Chartered Surveyors.. 195
The Worshipful Company of Chartered Accountants 197
The Worshipful Company of Chartered Secretaries and Administrators .. . 199
The Worshipful Company of Builders Merchants 201
The Worshipful Company of Launderers . .. .203
The Worshipful Company of Marketors 205
The Worshipful Company of Actuaries. 207
The Worshipful Company of Insurers 209
The Worshipful Company of Arbitrators . .. .211
The Worshipful Company of Engineers 213
The Worshipful Company of Fuellers 215
The Worshipful Company of Lightmongers 217
The Worshipful Company of Environmental Cleaners.. 219
The Worshipful Company of Chartered Architects. 221
The Worshipful Company of Constructors. 223
The Worshipful Company of Information Technologists . .. .225
The Worshipful Company of World Traders 227
The Worshipful Company of Water Conservators 229
The Worshipful Company of Firefighters. 231
The Worshipful Company of Hackney Carriage Drivers.. 233
The Worshipful Company of Management Consultants 235
The Worshipful Company of International Bankers 237
The Worshipful Company of Tax Advisers 239
The Worshipful Company of Security Professionals 241
The Worshipful Company of Parish Clerks. 243
The Company of Watermen and Lightermen. 245

Appendix I: Schedule of Dates of Masters' Badges 247
Appendix II: Grants of Arms to Livery Companies post 1954. 249

Select Bibliography.. 255

ACKNOWLEDGEMENTS

I am indebted to Noel Osborne (Master Stationer 2008-9) who readily offered the services of his publishing house if I could bring this project to fruition. The road to completion has been long and I have relied upon the help and advice of many, especially the Learned and Gallant Clerks and the Archivists of the various Worshipful Companies. In particular John Allen, Clerk to the Cutlers, has been a fount of knowledge and has put at my disposal his Company's unrivalled library of Company histories and its collection of badges of office and rank. I learned much from an interview with Grant Macdonald (Master Goldsmith 2008-9) at his workshop in Southwark on the background to the production of a Master's Badge, whilst Professor John Salter (Master Fan Maker 2008-9) has been kind enough to allow me to reproduce his vignettes on the various silversmiths who have been responsible for the crafting of the Badges. Securing photographs of sufficiently high resolution and with a consistency of background proved time consuming and I am grateful to Colin Middlemiss, Clerk of the Watermen & Lightermen, for readily allowing the use of Watermen's Hall for this purpose on more than one occasion. Andrew Illes spent much time on capturing these images and both he and Sarah Pavey, and all the staff at Phillimore & Co. Ltd have made my own task far easier that it might otherwise have been.

Mr C.E.A. Cheesman, Richmond Herald, helped me enormously in the preparation of Appendix II, ensuring that the Grants of Arms to the Livery Companies, post 1954, were accurately described.

However hard one tries there will always be errors and omissions and for these I alone am to blame.

Richard Goddard
(Master Waterman & Lighterman 2008-9)

Autumn 2011

INTRODUCTION

For those who have been privileged to attend grand Civic functions at the Mansion House or Guildhall or St Paul's, or indeed been present at dinners within the finery of the various Livery Halls, the overwhelming impression is one of grandeur and ceremony. The Lord Mayor and the Aldermen in their scarlet, the latter accompanied by their Ward Beadles in uniforms dazzling in blue or green and gold, the Sheriffs with their magnificent triple chains of office and the Masters, Prime Wardens and Upper Bailiff each resplendent in colourful or sombre livery gowns and bedecked with a Chain of Office from which is pendant a glittering jewel vibrant with colourful heraldic display. These are scenes of medieval splendour; or so it would seem.

When I joined this circuit as a Master I was especially bowled over by the magnificence of some of the Masters' Badges and sought in vain for a reference work that could shed some light on their provenance. Finding none, I was encouraged to undertake the work of producing such a volume myself.

I have been fortunate in the assistance that has been made available to me, so it is especially frustrating to have to admit that I am no nearer offering a clear and unequivocal answer to the most frequently asked question, namely, when did Masters first wear a Badge of Office? What I can say is that it was certainly not a medieval practice but probably started among two or three Companies at about the same time that the livery badge was introduced on an *ad hoc* basis in the third quarter of the 18th century. The oldest badge still worn by a Master is that of the Distillers, dating from 1852. Further than that is mere conjecture. What can be asserted without contradiction is that there was a flowering of badges between 1860 and 1890 and that today every Company is in possession of a Master's Jewel. And what jewels they are! A Master Draper told me that when he was invested with his badge his predecessor murmured, 'Now you will know how a woman feels' and when asked to elucidate was told, 'People will be staring at your chest throughout every dinner you attend!' Take a look at the photograph of the Drapers' badge glittering with diamonds and you will understand the veracity of that comment.

I had thought of giving as title to this work a line from Gray's Elegy, namely,

'The boast of heraldry, the pomp of power'

only to remember, in time, how the stanza ended:

'And all that beauty, all that wealth e'er gave
Awaits alike the inevitable hour
The paths of glory lead but to the grave.'

Rather too apt a sentiment for us Past Masters, I fear!

There are many apocryphal stories circulating about the badges, including frequent tales of their temporary loss in bizarre circumstances by errant Masters. Memories can be fallible and wherever possible I have tried to check, either with the printed Company history or, if practicable, with the primary sources of the Company Minutes. Nonetheless, 'folk memory' often provides a valuable insight into a new line of enquiry and further information is sure to come to light and it would be very helpful if any new facts could be reported so that these could be integrated into the data already on file. This is especially the case with respect to the names of the silversmiths whose skills have given us this precious heritage: we possess a truly remarkable collection of jewels, many masterpieces of the silversmiths' and the goldsmiths' arts – they deserve to be documented accurately, as well as cherished and celebrated.

The Right Honourable The Lord Mayor
Alderman David Wootton

It is surprising that the history and development of the Badges of Office of the Masters, Prime Wardens and Upper Bailiff of the City Livery Companies has remained unexplored for so long: having identified this omission Richard Goddard has produced this excellent work which admirably redresses the gaps in our knowledge and in addition gives us tales galore of lost and stolen badges, of badges destroyed in the Blitz and of those so precious that they never leave their Halls.

Beyond this original research, the particular joy of this book is the Badges themselves, captured in full colour and brought together in one volume for the very first time. It is a wonderful record of our Companies' heritage spanning 200 years.

I am most grateful to Richard Goddard for his initiative and hard work. I commend this book to all Liverymen and indeed to all those who delight in beautiful artefacts and craftsmanship of the highest quality.

ILLUSTRATION ACKNOWLEDGEMENTS

All photographs are taken by Andrew Illes except for the following which have been kindly provided by:

Worshipful Company of Barbers, p.10
Worshipful Company of Chartered Accountants, p.14, p.15
Worshipful Company of Clothworkers, p.4, p.5
The Worshipful Company of Firefighters, p.230
The Worshipful Company of Framework Knitters, p.152
The Worshipful Company of Glaziers and Painters of Glass, p.130
Guild of Air Pilots and Air Navigators, p.23
Peter Holt, p.218
Grant Macdonald Silversmiths, p.206, p.238
Philip McCarthy, p.-72
Sarah Pavey, p.146, p.164
The Worshipful Company of Skinners, p.38
SMS Creative Photography, p.196
The Worshipful Company of Upholders, p.122
Worshipful Company of Vintners, p.2
Based upon illustration in *Coat-Armour of the London Livery Company* (Welch, 1914), p.21
All images in Appendix II taken from the Livery Companies' Website, hosted by the Worshipful Company of Fishmongers.

LIST OF SUBSCRIBERS

*Subscribers are listed exactly as they indicated on the order form, and subscriptions from
Livery Companies are included alphabetically by Company name.*

Brian Adair
Geoff Adams
Dr Donald Adamson
John Alexander (Chartered Accountant
	and Past Master, Tobacco Pipe Makers
	and Tobacco Blenders)
David Allen
John Allen
G. Anthony Alton (Past Master, Tobacco
	Pipe Makers and Tobacco Blenders)
Maurice Avent
Paul Baldwin
Nigel Bamping
The Worshipful Company of Barbers
Brian Barker QC
Deputy Doug Barrow
Dr David Bartle
The Worshipful Company of Basketmakers
John Baxter
Professor Trevor Beedham
P.F.B. Beesley
Michael J. Bellis (Past Master Baker)
Sir Christopher Benson DL
David Bentata (Past Master Feltmaker)
Jeffrey Bines
Mr Raymond G. Blaber
Admiral Sir Jeremy Black GBE KCB DSO
Mrs Steven Blair
David Blake JP
Mark Blandford-Baker
Geoffrey C. Bond OBE DL FSA
Mr Robert John Bould (Master of
	Worshipful Company of Chartered
	Surveyors, 2010-11)
Stephen Bourne
J.H. Bowman
The Brewers' Company
Michael Broadway
G.P. Brocklebank
Rodney D. Brody
C.J. Brown
Mrs Sue Brownson OBE (Master of the
	Worshipful Company of Coach and
	Coachharness Makers)
Peter Brunner
The Worshipful Company of
	Builders Merchants

Richard Callingham
Paul Campion
John Carpenter
The Carpenters' Company
Rodney Cartwright
Colonel George Edward Cauchi CBE DL
Sir Peter Cazalet
Arthur E.W. Chapman
Bertram Chapman
John Chard
Anthony Charlwood
The Worshipful Company of Chartered
	Secretaries and Administrators
George T. Chudley
Nigel Churton
Mrs Sarah Clark
Graham Clarke
Sir Anthony Cleaver
The Clothworkers' Company
David Cole-Adams
Captain Jim Conybeare
The Cook & The Butler Event Company
Mr Robert Constant
Mr Brian Coombe
Brian J. Coombe
The Worshipful Company of Coopers
The Worshipful Company
	of Cordwainers
Dr Derek C. Cornish
Alan W. Cornwell
T.S. Corrigan OBE
Mr Jeremy D. Courtney
The Worshipful Company of Cutlers
John Dallimore
Dr Ian Daniell (Worshipful Company of
	Management Consultants)
Martin Davies
Captain A.P.M. Davis
Professor Martyn P. Davis
Michael D. Davis
Michael H. Davis
Peter Doe
Robin Doran (Past Master,
	Plaisterers' Company)
The Drapers' Company
Harry F. Druce (Master, Worshipful
	Company of Marketors, 1989)

Mr Ian Drury
J. Anthony Dunn
The Dyers' Company
John C. Edgcumbe
David Eking
Sir Jeremy Elwes
Peter Esslemont
The Worshipful Company of Fan Makers
Alastair Farley
The Worshipful Company of Farmers
The Worshipful Company of Farriers
The Worshipful Company of Firefighters
Brian D. Fishwick
Nicholas John Fiske
Philip Fortey
Charles R.S. Fowler TD DL FCA
Alan French
The Worshipful Company of
	Furniture Makers
Keith Gabriel (Past Prime Warden,
	Blacksmiths' Company)
The Worshipful Company of Gardeners
Hugh Garforth-Bles
Stephen Nicholas Jonathan Gee
Emma-Jane C. Gilbart-Smith
Michael S. Gilham
Walter Gill (Worshipful Company
	of Carmen)
Richard Gillis
George M.F. Gillon
The Worshipful Company of Girdlers
The Worshipful Company of Glaziers
	and Painters of Glass
David Goddard
Jonathan E. Godrich
J.A. Simmons (Past Master, Gold and
	Silver Wyre Drawers)
Tony Gordon-James
Peter Winwood Gossage
Jeremy Gotch KStJ
Harold Gould OBE JP DL
Mark Gower-Smith
Ian Mitchell Grimshaw
The Worshipful Company of Grocers
Julie S. Gubbins
The Worshipful Company of
	Haberdashers

The Worshipful Company of Hackney
   Carriage Drivers
Alan V. Hall
Peter Hamblin
H.J.W. Harman
Rear Admiral N.H.L. Harris CB MBE
David Hattersley
Eileen N. Hawkes
J.C. Hayes
Christopher Hayman
W.I. Head
Nicholas Heal
Chris Heaps (Past Master Worshipful
   Company of Curriers, 1997-8)
Lt Col Peter Henderson OBE (Clerk to
   The Coachmakers)
Paul Herbage
Jonathan Hill
K.S.G. Hinde
Mr Nigel J. Hollebone
Prof. David W. Holt
Jeffrey Hordle
John A. Howard
Chris P. Hudson
M.A. Hudson
Martin Humphrys JP
W.G. Hunt TD BA FCA
John C. Hutchins
Capt. Bruce Hutton (Guild of Air Pilots
   and Air Navigators)
Keith Hutton
Andrew Illes
David Ingmire
The Clerk, The Worshipful Company
   of Innholders
The Worshipful Company of Ironmongers
Nigel Israel FSA
Edward A. Jackson
Rory Jackson
Michael Jeans
Roy L. Jennings
Laurence Johnstone
Graham F. Jones
Neville A. Joseph
Sir Paul Judge
William Kennair
Paul M. Kennerley
Colonel David King OBE (Clerk,
   Worshipful Company of Farmers)
Terence Douglas King (Master,
   Worshipful Company of
   Environmental Cleaners, 1997-8)
His Honour Dr Colin Kolbert
   (Master Wax Chandler, 2009-10)
Brian S. Lamden FRICS
Robert Lampitt
Simon V. Langton
Professor John Last CBE
Christopher J.F. Latham
The Worshipful Company of Launderers
The Worshipful Company
   of Leathersellers
Clive W. Lidstone MBE
Philip Linnell
Alderman Ian Luder
J.B. Lumsden
Mr J.K. Lyden OBE
Peter Maplestone (Past Master, Parish
   Clerks)
Alexandra Marks
William Marle
William Marle
Edward H. Marlow
David Marwood
Richard Martin
Richard C. Martin
The Worshipful Company of Masons
Jason Vincent McCreanney
Michael McDowell

Christopher McKane (Master Stationer,
   2010-11)
Angus Menzies (Honourable Company
   of Master Marineres)
Merchant Taylors' Company
Colin Middlemiss
Derek Glanvile Millard
Anthony R. Miller RD*
John Miller
Margaret M. Miller
John Mills
Richard Model
Robert A. Moore
Professor John Morehen
Fr Derek Mottershead
Dr Jonathan Munday JP
John C.R. Naylor
The Worshipful Company
   of Needlemakers
Richard Nevard
Brian G. Newell
Donald Newell (Past Master Pattenmaker)
Chas G. Newens
Canon Nigel Nicholson
M.W.D. Northcott
Hugh Ogus (Past Master Lightmonger)
Tim Oliver (Master Ironmonger, 2002)
M. Osborne
Noel Osborne (Master Stationer,
   2008-9)
Stephen Osborne
Gp Capt D. Packman
The Worshipful Company of
   Painter-Stainers
Dr R.N. Palmer
Philip J. Panchaud
Canon David Parrott
Captain Malcolm W. Parrott
   (Past Master, 2009-10, HCMM)
Stephen Parsons
Lt Col R.J.A. Paterson-Fox
Sarah Pavey
Captain G.M. Pepper
Sir John Perring
The Worshipful Company of Pewterers
John E. Phillips
Tim Piper
M. Pitts
The Worshipful Company of Plaisterers
Stephen Plumb: Parish Clerk,
   St Christopher Le Stocks
The Master of the Worshipful Company
   of Plumbers
Alan Pontin
Michael J. Poulter
David Powell
Mark Powell
Mr Chris Price (Master Engineer, 2009-10)
Richard V. Proctor
Jeremy Randall
Chrisopher Basil Ratcliffe
John Ray
Francis Read (Master, The Worshipful
   Company of Barbers, 2007-8)
Alderman Neil Redcliffe
David Redwood
Colin Reese QC
Jessica Reeve
Dominic Reid OBE
Dr Iain Reid
Keith Riddle
Peter Roberts (Cutlers' Company)
Peter D.T. Roberts
Angus Robertson
John Rushton (Master, Worshipful
   Company of Arbitrators, 2008-9)
The Worshipful Company of Saddlers
Professor John R. Salter
Michel Saminaden

Martin L.H. Sankey
Captain Martin Scott
Roy Scott JP MD FRCS DL
The Worshipful Company of Scriveners
Richard L. Seaman
Ian C.N. Seaton (Master Girdler, 2008-9)
Lawrence Paul Shapiro GSWD
Terrence Shapland
Mr E.F. Shawyer CBE
David Sherriff
The Worshipful Company of Shipwrights
Ronald J. Sichel
Roger N. Smaridge FCA
Dr Noel Snell
Sir Michael Snyder
John Spanner TD, CC
The Worshipful Company of
   Spectacle Makers
Captain Anthony Speed
Duncan Spence
Francis Spencer-Cotton
D.T. Spencer-Phillips
Mark Spofforth
C.W. Sprague
L.R. Springett
S.R. Springett
David Squires
Michael Squires
John L. Stace
T.E. Statham
Dr Christian Steinmann
Hugh Stevenson
Sir Alastair Stewart Bt
Mr G.H. Stow
Maurice J. Summerfield Hon. ARAM
Jim Surguy
Henry Tattersall
Judy Tayler-Smith
Enid Taylor
Dr Joanna Thomas
Nigel Thomson
Mr John G. Thorpe
John A. Townsend
Bryan E. Toye
Eric Tracey
Richard Tranter
The Worshipful Company of Tylers
   and Bricklayers
Christopher Twyman
Sir Lawrence and Lady Verney
Sir Roger Vickers KCVO
The Worshipful Company of Vintners
Robert Adrian Joseph Waddingham
H. Richard Walduck OBE JP DL KStJ
Sir Christopher Walford
Tim Waller
Mr N.J. Watson
Tim Watts
The Worshipful Company of
   Wax Chandlers
The Worshipful Company of Weavers
Alan C. Wells
Anthony West
Michael Peter West
Thomas Wheatley-Hubbard
John Brian Whitaker
Alderman John R.C. White TD
Mr Lance Whitehouse
Anthony Willenbruch
David Wills
W. Eric Wilson CBE (Master, The
   Worshipful Company of Woolmen)
Mrs Susan Wood
Martin C. Woods
Barry M. Woodman
Richard Woodman-Bailey (Master Mason)
Robert Woodward
Alderman Fiona and Mr Nicholas Woolf
Professor Graham Zellick CBE QC

PART I

I

How it all began

During the early days of the City Guilds the mark of distinction for the senior members of the fraternity was the gown – the livery itself – after which was named this rank of membership. The Master and Wardens of the guild would often be distinguished by robes enhanced with fur trimming, whilst some companies had installation ceremonies at which the Master and Wardens were adorned with crowns, garlands, caps, wreaths or bonnets,[1] although it seems that the wearing of such headgear was confined to high days in the Guild's year. At other times, the Master would usually be escorted by an official bearing a staff of office (sometimes, less accurately, called a mace) and a number of these that still exist are of some antiquity.[2] By the 18th century the wearing of badges by Company servants had also become long established. In particular the Company's Bargemaster would be furnished with a large silver badge, emblazoned with the Company's Arms and worn upon the upper left arm. The Cordwainers possess a Bargemaster's Badge c.1580 and there is any number from the 17th and 18th centuries (Brewers 1667, Drapers 1671).[3] It seems likely that this practice was then adopted by some of the Companies' Beadles and certainly the Cordwainers' Bargemaster's Badge, mentioned above, is now worn by their Beadle.

In Medieval and Tudor times the wearing of livery was commonplace amongst Royal retainers and the followers of a nobleman or by members of a fraternity, but by the 18th century it was regarded as the uniform of the servant classes and accordingly its use by liverymen of the City's Worshipful Companies fell out of favour.

It is known that there were several attempts to insist upon liverymen wearing their livery gowns at Common Hall during the late 1700s but such pleas fell, for the most part, on deaf ears. To assist those seeking to authenticate the identity of those properly entitled to vote at Guildhall a number of Companies introduced a medal to be worn by their liverymen. Probably the custom was first instituted by the Vintners in 1769[4] although the Vintners' own notes on their Company Insignia state 'they [livery badges] were instituted in 1771 to be used as tickets for entrance into the Hall on feast days'.

---

1   Such apparel was worn by, among others, the Apothecaries, Skinners, Plumbers, Girdlers, Carpenters. The Cooks continue the practice to the present day.
2   The Weavers mention a Beadle's staff from c.1500, Mercers' staves date from 1679 and those of the Needlemakers and the Bakers predate 1700. There are several from the 18th century.
3   *Ceremonial Badges on the River Thamse* by Kenneth Nicholls Palmer.
4   *A Badge of Rank* by Herbert, Hinde and Salter.

Possibly the first
Master's Badge
(Vintners, c.1700).

Whatever the original intention of the Vintners, the practice was rapidly followed, between 1770 and 1775, by several other Companies,[5] though as a means of controlling voting it was an experiment that was less than successful in achieving its goal and was relatively short-lived as an electoral tool; although the use of livery medals within Companies had a far longer usage and, of course, persists to the present day as a means of identifying this rank of membership.

Nonetheless, an interesting development flowed from the livery medal. Some Companies extended and refined the practice of all liverymen wearing an identifying token by introducing rules requiring members of the Court and especially the Master to wear such medals as badges of rank or office.

Here, again, it seems the Vintners were to the forefront of this innovation. In the descriptions of the Company's insignia, reference is made to a badge which, 'although unmarked, can be dated stylistically to roughly the third quarter of the 17th century … It has been worn by the Immediate Past Master since 1930, but was probably originally the Master's Badge, until supplanted in 1878 …'.[6]

There is no hard evidence of when this jewel was first worn by the Master as a Badge of Office, or indeed if it were ever so employed. However, it is a reasonable conjecture that the Vintners had the notion of devising a medal for their liverymen based upon the design of the existing badge worn by their Master.

For those Companies which, during the closing decades of the 18th century, adopted the practice of identifying the Master by a special badge, that sequence was reversed. In December 1771 the Court Minutes of the Pattenmakers recorded: 'The Master for the time being to ware [*sic*] the Great Medal and every other Member to ware [*sic*] his medal during the Court sitting …'.[7] This latter medal is almost certainly the livery medal which the Company had commissioned in March of the same year. In 1777 (or perhaps 1778) the Court of the Needlemakers commissioned silver-gilt medals for the Court. Clearly the Master would have worn one but it is not recorded if this were specifically as Master, although circumstantial evidence seems to suggest that a special badge might have been reserved for his use, for, in 1800, when Sutton Sharpe was elected Master, his name and the date were inscribed over an earlier name which had been erased. This medal is now in the Company's possession.[8]

The current badge of the Innholders' Middle Warden is inscribed 'The Gift of Mr John Pearson, Master 1789, to the Worshipful Company of Innholders, London' (hallmarked *c.*1784). Again, there is no documentary evidence that it was once worn by the Master but the inference can reasonably be made.

However, beyond the Vintners, Pattenmakers, Innholders and Needlemakers, there seems to be very little evidence that the practice of Masters adopting badges as a mark of office gained any popularity during the latter part of the 18th and the early 19th

---

5   S.A. Gilbert, writing in the *British Numismatic Journal*, 1931-3, states that he had only discovered 12 or 13 companies issuing livery medals during this period.

6   Vintners' Notes on Company Insignia.

7   *History of the Pattenmakers' Company.*

8   Letter from Geoffrey Selwyn (Needlemaker).

centuries. To some extent this is surprising, as the example of the Lord Mayor was readily observable by all the Livery and he had had a pendant to be suspended from the collar of SS (which itself was worn from at least 1544) since 1558 (albeit this was replaced in 1607 by the badge which is substantially the same as that worn to the present day). In 1849 it is related that Queen Victoria even decreed that municipal Mayors throughout the country should wear scarlet robes and a collar of office.[9] Be that as it may, the next reference to a Badge of Office amongst the Livery Companies seems to be in 1841 when the Clothworkers[10] had four circular medals bearing the Company's arms cast from a die made by Benjamin Wyon. Two were in gold and two in silver gilt and it seems that one was originally used by the Master and the others by the Wardens. During the years 1842 to 1859 further badges were struck and supplied to Masters whose names were engraved upon the reverse – in effect acting as Master's Badge in the year of office and denoting the position of Past Master in subsequent years. However, in 1860 the original 1841 badge was returned to the Company and it became the official Master's Badge of the Clothworkers till it was superseded by the 'Lambert' Badge of 1872.[11]

In 1852, a similar styled gold medal – this one an oval – was produced for the Distillers' Company, bearing the representation of a bust of their founder and on the obverse a rendition of the Company's arms. It was worn by Masters till the early 1980s when it was lost; now happily recovered, it is once more the badge of the Master Distiller and can be viewed [below at p.163] under this heading.

Just two years later, in 1854, the Minutes of the Dyers' Company record that the Court inaugurated gold medals for Past Prime Wardens and the badge currently worn by the Prime Warden certainly has a simplicity of form that would indicate an early provenance. Indeed, issuing badges to Past Masters can apparently be dated to at least 1823, as there is extant a circular gold medal bearing the arms of the Saddlers' Company and on the reverse the inscription 'GEORGE BISHOP MASTER 1823'. However, a note of caution needs to be sounded as 'it will be noted that the date on some of the badges is anterior to the date of issue.'[12] But similar badges were soon to be issued by the Salters and the Joiners (1850), Fishmongers (1852),[13] Coachmakers (1855) and Butchers (1857).[14] What is surprising is that this badge of rank seems to predate most Master's Badges, for surely it seems logical that if past holders of the office were to be so distinguished then the actual incumbent ought to have had a badge as well. Strangely there is scant reference to such badges in the Companies' Minutes. For instance, a new Clerk was appointed by the Joiners in 1852 and upon taking office a full inventory of all the deeds, documents and possessions of the Company was recorded in the Minute Book. There is reference to the Beadle's Staff and Gown, the Company's Great Seal and the Master's Gown but no reference whatsoever to a Master's, let alone Past Masters', Badges. Moreover, these same Minute Books make reference each year to a vote of thanks being passed on the

---

9   Reference City of Bath website.

10   Garnett (*see* 4 above) states that [Clothworkers'] '"wardens" badges were issued from 1841 to 1846 inclusive, then withdrawn'.

11   Correspondence from Jessica Collins, Archivist, Clothworkers' Company.

12   *City Livery Badges*, S.A. Garnett, 1931-3.

13   However, the Fishmongers' Curator thinks that the period when badges were issued to Past Masters seems to have been between 1861 and 1882.

14   *Handbook of the Collections. Part 1 Worshipful Company of Cutlers.*

Master demitting his office but, again, there is no record of him being invested with a Past Master's Badge.[15] In some Companies, the sequence might have been that the livery badge was gilded (or replaced by a badge in gold) upon accession to the Court and, like the Cooks until at least 1893, this was augmented with a bar denoting the date of service as Master.[16] Alternatively, perhaps, at this period the principal means of identifying the Master remained a distinctive gown and, on leaving office, it was felt appropriate to offer some acknowledgement for the services that had been rendered to the Company by the award of a badge. Whatever the reasons it is frustrating that so much of the early history of the Master's Badge has to be conjecture and sometimes one has to reply upon 'negative evidence', as in the statement of an archivist of the Mercers who wrote in 1953: 'I cannot find any evidence that there was ever any earlier Master's Badge [pre 1871] as none is mentioned in the inventories of 1616, 1685 or 1741.'[17]

Interestingly not every Company settled on a badge to commemorate a Past Master's service as Master – in 1890 a Committee of the Basketmakers recommended to the Court that 'Past Officers'

The Master's Badge of the Clothworkers' Company, dating from 1841.

Mementos should take the form of a badge at a cost not exceeding 2 gns each' but this was referred back and at a subsequent Court it was 'proposed and seconded that gentlemen who have filled the office of Prime Warden to this date be presented with a silver salver of the pattern selected with a suitable inscription'.[18]

Reverting to early badges: the three Master's Badges of the Clothworkers, the Distillers and the Dyers are certainly atypical in design when compared with those badges that came later, and indeed the next badge to have been identified by date is the elaborate and elegant badge of the Merchant Taylors, which bears an inscription dating it to 1857 and sets the pattern for most future badges – that is to say it is a representation in pierced gold and enamel of the full achievement of the Company's arms (albeit that the original badge was augmented by the addition of a scroll frame some twenty years later).

Then, over the next two decades, there came a veritable explosion in the introduction of badges for Masters, so much so that by 1871 it can be recorded: 'The Master [Pewterer] and Wardens accepted an invitation from His Royal Highness [probably The Prince of Wales, as he was President of Her Majesty's Commissioners of the Exhibition] in April 1871 to attend the opening of the International Exhibition in London' and at the next meeting of the Court of the Company it was 'moved that a committee be appointed to consider the propriety of providing a suitable badge or

---

15   Minutes of the Joiners & Ceilers (1850-5).

16   *See* 10 above.

17   Note from Archivist to Clerk of the Mercers, 1953.

18   Minutes of the Basketmakers' Company, 1890 (Guildhall Library).

medal for the Master to wear on State occasions' – presumably the Master had felt under-dressed amongst his peers! Who knows but the same Royal occasion might have prompted the Mercers' Court in April 1871 to minute: 'The attention of the Court having been drawn to the desirability of having some distinguishing Badge of Office for the Master of the Company to wear on public occasions it was resolved that the same be provided at a cost not to exceed £100.'[19] Similar Minutes abound – in 1873 the Court of the Clockmakers commented on 'the desirability of providing a Badge for the Master', in the following year the Farriers' Court recorded that 'it had been necessary that a proper badge should be executed for the Master and Wardens'. In 1877 the Master Gunmaker informed his Court 'that most Masters of City Companies had a Badge of Office and he considered the Gunmakers' Company should have one, and he had had one made, which he duly presented to the Company';[20] whilst as late as 1892 the Court of the Carmen 'became aware that there was no Master's Badge and the Clerk reported that a simple one could be made for 10 guineas' and one was indeed made in gold and enamel and it is recorded that this represented 'a glimmer of the old pride in Fellowship'.[21]

Obviously, when several Companies provided badges for their Masters, it acted as a spur to the rest. The dates of this growth in splendid display are also of significance. First, they corresponded with the renaissance of many Companies that had become moribund. The Fan Makers, for example, maintain that the creation of the Master's Badge in 1878 coincided with the revitalisation of the Company and the increase in the number of its livery, whilst the Needlemakers replaced their earlier badge in 1874 – the new jewel being commissioned after the 'revival of the Company by gentlemen of substance'. Put another way, 'in the 1870s came what one Company historian termed "the great awakening"'.[22]

Of course, these decades also saw the Livery Companies under attack from Government, whilst the long drawn out deliberations of various Royal Commissions also had the effect of persuading the Companies to assert their rights and privileges and what better way of 'celebrating [their] sense of corporate splendour [than] by buying a gold and enamel badge for the Master.'[23] The Coopers commissioned a new Hall in 1869 which inspired the Company to review its traditions and their badge followed in 1872. A recent history of the Armourers and Brasiers records, 'The increased revenue [generated] and perhaps too a certain rise in self-awareness caused by the public attacks [on the Livery] had other effects and in 1875 the company commissioned a splendid Master's Badge'.[24]

---

19 Note prepared for the Mercers' Clerk in 1953.
20 *The Worshipful Company of Gunmakers: A History* (2008).
21 *Carr and Carmen* (1999).
22 *The City of London and its Livery Companies*.
23 *The History of the Gold and Silver Wyre Drawers*.
24 *Use of Metal* (2008).

Suffice it to say that by the dawn of the 20th century virtually every Master, Prime Warden and Upper Bailiff had a Badge of Office and most Companies had badges for their Wardens as well. Some had a chain or collar to which the badge could be attached when the Master was in robes. Whilst badges and chains were often commissioned by the Court, sometimes at the Company's expense though occasionally by a subscription from the Court Assistants, it became more and more the convention for these to be the gift of a Past Master and this led to the practice of earlier badges being superseded by a more elaborate version (with the original usually being assigned to the Immediate Past Master, Deputy Master or a Warden); alternatively some badges were augmented with jewelled borders (as with the Tallow Chandlers, the Cordwainers, the Farriers and the Gunmakers) or by some other 'improving' addition.

On rare occasions, and in more recent times, one finds that the badge was the gift of an outside agency, albeit one with a close or symbiotic relationship with the Company: so the Insurers' Master's Badge, together with those of the Wardens, were the gift of the committee of the Corporation of Lloyds in 1980 and the Lightmongers' Badge was purchased in 1983 from a donation made by the Board of Directors of ASEE Exhibitions Ltd.

Some gifts were associated with a particular event of a national nature, as, for example the Golden and the Diamond Jubilees of Queen Victoria, the Coronations of Edward VII and George V; or of an occurrence specific to the Company itself, as, say, the 600th Anniversary of the Carpenters' Company, the 500th anniversary of the Bakers' or the 300th of the Tin Plate Workers'. Sometimes the gift was to commemorate a change to, or amplification of, a grant of arms and these are discussed in more detail below.

In 1926, after a gap of 217 years, a new Company joined the ranks of the Livery and in keeping with the traditions of their fellows the Master Mariners provided their Master with a badge – and what a badge! The work of Omar Ramsden, it is a remarkable example of the silversmiths' art and is more fully discussed in a later chapter. The Honourable Company was followed by 30 other companies, all of which have insignia for their Masters and there is now no Company without a Badge of Office.

In this respect it might be worth considering the case of the Grocers' Company, as historically the Master never wore a badge. 'Indeed it is said that the absence of a badge was one of the distinguishing marks of the Master Grocer. This changed for good following the destruction by fire of the fourth Grocers' Hall in 1965. To mark the opening of the fifth Hall in 1970 on the same ancient site, the other eleven of the Great Twelve Livery companies commissioned a badge for the Master.'[25]

In virtually every instance the badge takes as its principal constituent a representation of the Company's coat of arms. Although prominent, very occasionally the arms are not always the dominant feature. So, when seeing the Fan Makers' Badge for the first time it is the fan itself (as a background to the coat of arms) that makes the impact. Similarly the Upholders' new badge, commissioned in 2000 to commemorate the millennium, depicts the Company's arms on a cushion. The badges created by Grant Macdonald for the Tax Advisers and for the Actuaries break new ground. They are in three dimensions, the former depicting coins cascading from a medieval money purse, the latter showing the representation of an hour glass in gold. Both display their respective coats of arms but it is the impact of the modelled object that seizes one's attention.

---

25   Letter from the Clerk, Brigadier R. Pridham, OBE.

Just a glance at the ensuing photographs will give ample evidence that many of the Masters' Badges are jewels of great worth, not only artistically but intrinsically as well. There are some badges with values now in the tens, even the hundreds, of thousands of pounds and this has led to the practice of secondary or 'Travelling' Badges being commissioned so that the exceedingly valuable original can remain within the Hall and hence is only worn at internal functions. Sometimes a particular incident prompts the manufacture of a replica, as seems to have been the case with the Mercers, who in the 1970s had a great scare when their badge was left in a taxi. They investigated the costs of producing a Travelling Badge using synthetic rubies and white sapphires to replicate the rubies and diamonds of the 1871 original.

Other duplicates are similarly facsimiles rendered in a less precious metal, so the Girdlers' Badge is 18ct gold and the Travelling Badge is in silver gilt. The Stationers put it more bluntly by describing the second version as 'a cheaper facsimile'. Sometimes an earlier Master's Badge now serves the function of a Travelling Badge, as with the Carpenters: whilst the Omar Ramsden badge of 1933 remains within the Hall its 1871 predecessor goes out with the Master. The Goldsmiths had that in mind for their 1948 badge when it was replaced in 1953 but it was eventually considered 'too large and of dated appearance' properly to fulfil the role and a purpose-made Travelling Badge was commissioned in 1994 from Lexi Dick. Some of the modern Companies also have Travelling Badges, as, for example, the Engineers and the Chartered Surveyors.

These second badges are sometimes known by different names, so the Butchers have a 'Day Badge' and the Basketmakers an 'Undress Badge' and presumably both offer a clue as to when and with what garb the various badges are deployed. Certainly the Fishmongers use the 'Wood' Badge only when the Prime Warden wears a double-stranded gold chain on special occasions such as Election Day[26] within the Hall.

For security reasons it is probably imprudent to ascribe specific present-day values to particular badges but it is historically fascinating to consider the prices that were originally paid. Naturally the wealth of a Company determined just how much it was willing to expend but notwithstanding these variables it is interesting to remark that the badges commissioned by the Courts during the period 1870 to 1890 were all purchased within a reasonably narrow price range. Of the 17 badges for which we have a cost price, 15 fell between 14 guineas and £75, with only the Mercers and the Leathersellers striding ahead at £125 and £120 respectively.

Some very generous donors greatly exceeded these figures, with the Tallow Chandlers receiving the gift of an additional border of diamonds to their existing badge from a Past Master at a cost well in excess of £200.

Rendering these prices into modern-day values is a rather imprecise science. There is any number of multipliers that can be applied: some refer to the increase in the Retail Price Index, others use a comparison of relative wages or salary rates.[27] For instance, when using RPI, a figure of £10 in 1870 would represent £713 at 2010 prices, whilst that same £10 would become some £5,900 if based upon increases in average earnings! Therefore, employing one multiplier based on prices, the average cost of a Master's Badge (£55 in the period 1870-90) would equate to £3,900 today, whereas using the

---

26   Correspondence with Claire Crawford, curator of the Fishmongers' Company.
27   MeasuringWorth.com website.

wage comparison it would become a striking £32,450. Actually, an average of these figures is probably not too far from the current-day valuations of the badges. We know, for instance, that a badge commissioned in 1984 cost £2,875 + VAT and it is also on record that other badges have insurance valuations that range from a modest £10,000 to some quite astronomical figures.

II

SILVERSMITHS AND DESIGNERS

The consideration of their value and their stylistic and design features brings one naturally to a discussion of the craftsmen who created them and the names of certain silversmiths are especially associated with the production of Masters' Badges. During the first hectic round of commissioning in the decades between 1860 and 1890, none is more frequently found than that of Lamberts of Coventry Street, Piccadilly, London W. Although the family business was founded in 1803, when Francis Lambert (born 1778) returned from Lisbon to establish a shop at 11 & 12 Coventry Street for the sale of jewellery and the manufacture of silver plate, it was not until after 1861 that, under the control of Francis's son, George, the firm's involvement with livery insignia developed. They produced the badges for the Pewterers (1871), Mercers (1871), Clothworkers (1872), Armourers (1875), Barbers (1877), Vintners (1878), and Curriers (1884), and when they merged in 1916 with Harman & Co. to become Harman & Lambert they made the Leathersellers' badge. As details of the provenance of many badges are scanty this cannot be considered an exhaustive list of their output and, in any event, it is perhaps surprising that George Lambert persevered with livery work in the light of his experiences when dealing with his commission from the Pewterers. Their Court had agreed to supply badges for the Master and the Wardens provided the total cost did not exceed £20 – an earlier proposal that the cost should not exceed £10 having been rejected! At a later meeting the Upper Warden showed two designs for a Master's Badge, one costing £17.10.0 and the other £20. In view of these costs the Wardens agreed to forego their badges and it was agreed to order the Master a badge at £20. In November a letter was received from Mr Lambert, the gist of which is as follows: 'with respect to the price of the badge which we have just manufactured … we find it impossible to work the badge as we intended [at the agreed price] … and we trust that you in your munificence permit us to charge and be paid the amount mentioned in our bill rendered …' Later the Court agreed to pay £22.[1]

---

1   Pewterers' Court Book entries.

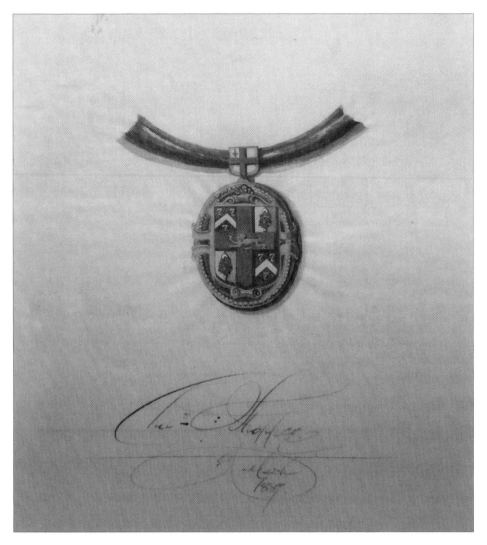

C.J. Shoppee's design for Master's Badge (Barbers' Company Minute Book).

Interestingly, two badges that can be traced to the work of Lambert – those for the Armourers and Brasiers and the Barbers – were both designed by Charles John Shoppee (b.1823, d.1897), who was at various times Master of both Companies; he was also responsible for the design of the Turners' badge. He was an architect and surveyor with an antiquarian bent and an extensive collection of objects of artistic and archaeological interest that were housed in a museum in his house.[2] He was a founder member of the Ex Libris Society devoted to the study and collection of bookplates. His design for the Barbers' badge is retained in the Court Minute Book.

Indeed, in the early days it was not that unusual for the design of the badge to be undertaken by a member of the Court; a Mr Parker of the Clockmakers' Court laid his own design for a badge before the Court in 1873 and, as has been mentioned above

---

2   *Notable Barber-Surgeons* (2008).

the Master Gunmaker took it upon himself to have a badge made in 1877 and in 1879 Mr Brock Hunt, the Master Fletcher, produced a handsome silver gilt medal which he had struck appended to an appropriate ribbon for his use.

Two years later, in 1881, John Belcher, who was renowned for designing both the V & A Museum and the Institute of Chartered Accountants, took on the responsibility of devising the badge of the Curriers, of which Company he became Master in 1886. Although it is now exceedingly rare for such 'self-designing' to be encountered, it is interesting to note that the Founder Master of the Chartered Architects, John Reid (with his wife Sylvia) was responsible for designing the new Company's Master's Badge. John Reid was perhaps better known as Pageant Master of the City Corporation and, indeed, also designed the badge for that office. Finally, in 1991, when the World Traders were contemplating the form to be taken by their Master's Badge, they initiated a design competition. Their Master (The Earl of Limerick) was also Chancellor of the City of London Polytechnic, and he instigated the competition amongst the student of their Silversmithing and Jewellery department, from which the winning design by Miss Alexander Krikos was chosen.

However, the more usual practice has always been to employ established professional silversmiths and among the earliest identified with badge creation was the Wyon family. Benjamin (sometime chief engraver of Her Majesty's seals) produced the die from which the Master and Wardens' medallions were struck for the Clothworkers in 1841. The output of City of London medallions by the Wyons was prodigious and they went on to produce the 'Pretty' Badge for the Fishmongers' Prime Warden in 1877.

Smith & Nicholson of Duke Street, Lincoln's Inn Fields made silver from 1851 to 1864, exhibiting at the Great Exhibition of 1851 and devising the Merchant Taylors' Master's Badge in 1857.

Another silversmith prominent in badge creation was the firm of Hicklenton & Phillips, which is recorded as producing badges for the Ironmongers, Masons, Tallow Chandlers and Launderers. It was established in Queen Street before moving to Cheapside. A company with the same name continues to trade from Wimborne Minster, Bournemouth when the original firm was bought out after the death of Howard George Hicklenton. Two more firms that continue to trade and indeed supply badges to the City Companies to this day are Thomas Fattorini of Birmingham and Toye, Kenning & Spencer. The former was established in Yorkshire by Antonio Fattorini in 1827 but one of the branches decided to set up a dedicated factory in Birmingham to take advantage of the demand for badges and medals, primarily from newly established and flourishing sporting bodies, but especially from football clubs.[3] In the 20th and 21st centuries Fattorini (still led by a member of the family) has been responsible for the production of badges for the Bowyers, Carmen, Constructors, Water Conservators and (probably) Air Pilots and Air Navigators. The Toye family arrived in England in 1685, fleeing the punitive restrictions imposed on the Huguenots in France, and soon resumed the traditional family business of weaving and gold and silver wire making. In 1865 the firm began the production of regalia, especially that associated with Freemasonry. 'But Toye was not working in a vacuum – other firms were competing in the same marketplace, indeed the names of Spencer and Kenning were bywords in the business world in which

---

3   Facts taken from Thomas Fattorini Ltd – History (website entry).

Toye operated.' In 1801 Richard Spencer began trading in Masonic and ceremonial regalia whilst in the 1860s George Kenning set up his own firm specialising in regalia. Eventually amalgamation or absorption saw the company renamed as Toye, Kenning & Spencer, under which title it continues to trade today – indeed still under the leadership of Bryan Toye, a direct descendant of the original émigrés.[4] Badges for the Fletchers (from George Kenning & Co.), Chartered Surveyors, Engineers, Needlemakers and (probably) Solicitors, have all originated from this source.

During the first four decades of the 20th century probably the greatest designer of silver working in England was Omar Ramsden (born 1873, died 1939). In 1898 he and fellow silver designer Alwyn Carr set up in partnership in London to produce fine 'art' silver, exploiting the fashionable taste for handmade silver in the style of the Arts and Crafts movement, and often incorporating designs based on Gothic and Renaissance originals. Then, as the century progressed, Ramsden moved from designs inspired by the Art Nouveau movement to those derived from Art Deco. His remarkable prowess did not escape the notice of the Livery Companies, but only the deepest pockets or those prompted by the most exceptional motives could justify commissioning him to create a Master's Badge. Despite his exotic name, Ramsden was the son of a greengrocer from Sheffield. At 17 years of age he studied at the Sheffield School of Art and subsequently at the Royal College of Art in London. He and Carr entered their joint mark at Goldsmiths' Hall in 1898 and prospered from the outset. 'During the height of his career Omar Ramsden had been likened to Carl Fabergé. Like Fabergé, Ramsden was to gather together craftsmen of the highest calibre, but never as did Fabergé would he allow his employees to be personally identified with the pieces for which they were responsible.'[5] One of his masterpieces is the collar and jewel of the Master of the Honourable Company of Master Mariners. This Company, the first to be admitted to the Livery since 1709, desired suitably impressive regalia and through the munificence of Lord Rothermere they achieved their wish. Rothermere's son opined that his father's choice of Ramsden as designer was simply because he was the best available. As was the maker's habit, the reverse is inscribed, 'I was wrought by Omar Ramsden for the Honourable Company of Master Mariners by Command of the Right Honourable the Viscount Rothermere PC in the years of our Lord 1929-1930 to commemorate the distinction of HRH The Prince of Wales being the first Master …' Although there is no doubt Ramsden was the inspiration for the design, 'he was to play little or no part in the practical execution of the work. The credit for this really belongs to William Maggs, his designer/draughtsman and the modelling to A.E. Ulyett, his workshop manager, assisted by the enameller Henri de Koningh.'[6]

A year or two later Ramsden was to receive another commission from a Livery Company when the Carpenters' Company was about to celebrate a notable date in its history, namely the 600th anniversary of the making of the 'Boke of Ordinances' in 1333. The elegant 18ct gold badge in the art deco style was delivered into the hand of the Master by HRH The Prince of Wales at a Banquet held on 22 March 1933. All this is inscribed on the reverse as well as the legend '*Fecit me arle et opera sua Omar Ramsden*'.

Just before the Second World War the Carmen commissioned a new badge and enlisted the skills of Archibald Russell (Lancaster Herald at the College of Arms) as designer,

---

4   Facts taken from Toye, Kenning & Spencer's website history of the company.

5   Quotation and other data from article by Captain J.D. Norie FRSA (Honourable Company of Master Mariners).

6   *See* 5 above.

though the manufacture was undertaken by Thomas Fattorini. Immediately after the war the College was again consulted, this time by the Farmers regarding their Master's Badge and this may well account for the similarity of design between the two.

In the second half of the 20th century a new name burst into the world of the silversmiths. Grant Macdonald started work in 1969 immediately after his diploma show at the Sir John Cass School of Art. Business flourished and by the mid-1970s he was starting to outgrow his premises and moved, first to Benjamin Street and subsequently to Bear Lane, Southwark. Amazingly, it is even reported that 'on occasions his company has ordered so much gold that it has had an effect on the price of this precious metal.' Although over 90 per cent of Grant Macdonald Limited's output is exported, he has undertaken a deal of work in the City of London, including more than 20 Sheriff's Badges and, of course, a number of Master's Badges as well.[7]

These include the Actuaries, Arbitrators, Security Professionals and the Tax Advisers, to name just a selection. It is fascinating to talk to Mr Macdonald about the processes involved in the creation of such a badge. His initial discussions with representatives of the Company (or, indeed Guild, for frequently this procedure may be embarked upon years before the organisation reaches livery status) explore the history of the trade or profession concerned. Then a detailed examination of the heraldry of the Company's Achievement of Arms is undertaken, quite often in collaboration with the College of Arms. There are then more prosaic, but nonetheless essential, considerations that will impinge upon the design. It must, for instance, be remembered that the finished badge will be 'of one size that must fit all': tall men and petite women alike. The length of any pre-existing ribbon, collar or chain must also be factored into the equation. Then there may be elements of symbolism, in addition to the coat of arms, that the Company wants to be incorporated. Finally there is the need for the badge to be easily recognisable and unique, and some have certainly become 'a talking piece', as for instance the medieval three-dimensional purse of the Tax Advisers. But, perhaps, that is not the final aspect to be discussed and debated with the commissioning Company: there is always the sensitive matter of enquiring about the available budget!

The next stage is the production of a selection of rough sketches in black and white; when the Company's preference has been established more formal coloured drawings are prepared. Some of the three dimensional designs have even necessitated the manufacture of a wooden model to ascertain that the badge will sit comfortably against the wearer's chest.

On receiving approval from the client the metalwork (either in gold, silver or other metal) is prepared in-house, as will any jewels that might form part of the design. Enamelling, on the other hand, is sent out to a specialist, of which there are just three in the country capable of the quality of work needed in such a prestigious object.

As mentioned above, badges are occasionally commissioned before the Company receives livery status and, to avoid the expense of having an entirely new badge made some Companies make sensible provision. So the Water Conservators' badge originally displayed a scroll bearing the title 'Company of Water Conservators' which was removed and replaced with one showing the legend: 'Worshipful Company …' when the time came.

It is of interest to note that when this work was already in proof form it was revealed that the Court of the Chartered Accountants was in the process of approving the design

---

7   From The Pearson Silver Collection: Biographies website.

GRANT MACDONALD
GOLDSMITHS · SILVERSMITHS · DESIGNERS
ESTABLISHED 1969

**Descriptions of designs submitted for the new
Masters Badge for the Worshipful Company of Chartered Accountants'**

Design A   The form of this design is taken from the three towers within the shield of the Company coat of arms. This three dimensional shape is very strong yet has a lightness to it. The hand painted enamel coat of arms is fixed within the three towers so they surround the arms in a protective way. This does have a practical use as the front edges of the towers shields the enamel badge from damage.

Design B   This design is based on the shape of a 20 Pence piece, a heptagon which represents money and I hope signifies the professional role of the members of the Company. The enamel badge is set within reducing heptagons making the badge some 1.5cm to 2.0cm in depth.

Design C   The design is again based on money, the shape as you will clearly see in the three quarter view are radiating coin sections complete with milled edges and raised dots from a pound coin. These strong sections contain the recessed enamelled coat of arms. The radiating look of the badge I hope shows that the Company is at the centre, surrounded by its members and their profession.

Grant Macdonald

THE QUEEN'S AWARDS
FOR ENTERPRISE
INTERNATIONAL TRADE
2008

50 Bear Lane London SE1 0UH
Telephone 020 7633 0278 · Facsimile 020 7261 0094
www.grantmacdonald.com

of a new badge for the Master of their Company. The Company had approached Grant Macdonald, who submitted three designs, which were considered by the Court on 11 October 2011. The decision was to opt for Design C, and, with the permission of the Company, the design and the descriptions are shown below.

Silversmiths have also received regular employment repairing damaged badges; indeed, some such work is an almost annual occurrence. The most common problems involve damage to the enamels, frequently caused by the badge 'bouncing' against the table edge during luncheons and dinners. Other problems arise when jewels become dislodged from their settings or, as with the gold acorn suspended from the Blacksmiths' badge, pendant

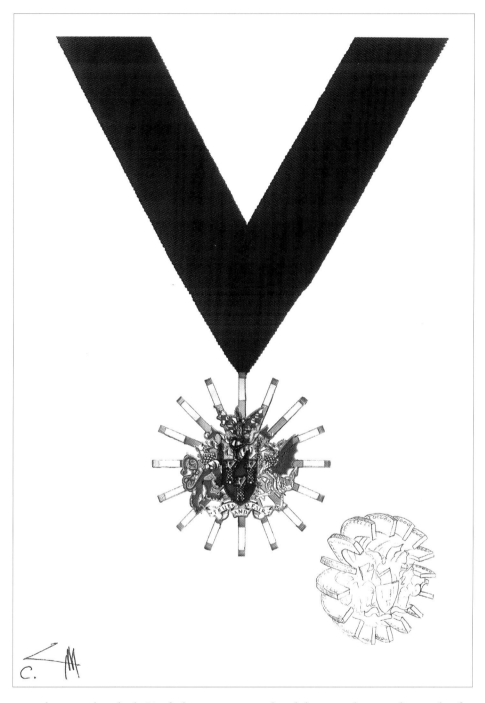

items become detached. Similarly, precious metalwork becomes bent or distorted – for these badges are worn with great frequency and are constantly being handled and not infrequently stuffed into pouches which are then consigned to a jacket pocket! All such remedial work, as with that relating to the creation of a new badge, requires meticulous attention to detail and such care and skill has been offered by all the many silversmiths who have, over the last 150 years, created these miniature works of art. The following list is by no means exhaustive but is the most complete that can currently be assembled from information provided by the various Companies. Sadly, in very many cases, the hallmarks, where they do exist, have been polished to such an extent that they are virtually illegible.

SILVERSMITHS AND DESIGNERS OF MASTER'S BADGES

Donald Abbott

Aspreys

George Attenborough & Son

Norman Bassant

John Belcher

Vince Bensson & Co.

Biden of Cheapside

Bradshaw & Co.

Brown & Co.

J.R. Brown

H.A. Byworth

John Bodman Carrington

Francis J.C. Cooper

John Gregory Crase

Lexi Dick

John Donald

Leslie G. Durbin

George Edwards

Maurice Emanuel

Thomas Fattorini

Garrards

George Gowland

Gowland Brothers, Cornhill

Harman & Lambert

Alan Henn

Hicklenton & Phillips

Sir David Hughes

Hunt & Roskill

George Kenning & Co.

A. Kimmance

R. & P. Kyte

Lambert & Co.

A.E. Lejune

George Lukes

Grant Macdonald

Percy Metcalf

Metcalf & Company

J.H. O'Dell

Omar Ramsden

Sylvia & John Reid

Searle & Co.

Charles Shoppee

Smith & Nicholson

Spencer of London

Spink & Son

Tessier

Cecil Thomas

David Thomas

David Tong

Toye, Kenning & Spencer

J.M. Willmin

Barry Witmond

J.S. & A.B. Wyon

HALLMARKS:

JWB

JB

RMW

JW&T

GK

D.S. & G.

TD

SJC

BMW

III

Lost, Stolen or Strayed

Considering that there are just 110 Company badges represented in this book (comprising those of 108 Livery Companies together with the Parish Clerks and the Watermen & Lightermen) it is a remarkable statistic that no fewer than 37 have been replaced for one reason or another. At least eight have been stolen; four have been lost, though all but one were subsequently recovered; five were damaged or destroyed in the Blitz; eight were replaced by newer versions that took account of alterations to the Company's heraldry and a further 12 were superseded for other considerations.

Looking at each category in more detail, let us consider those that were lost as a result of theft. In 1922 the Glass Sellers lost their badge and the replacement bears the inscription on the reverse: 'This badge was presented to the Worshipful Company of Glass-sellers [*sic*] by Past Master H. Marks to replace the one stolen during his year of office 1921-22'. Ten years later the Master Leatherseller reported that the badge had been stolen and a replica was ordered. On the other hand, when their Master reported his badge had been lost in a burglary in May 1955, the Fruiterers resolved not to produce an exact copy, even though there existed a plaster cast of the original, but rather decided to commission a new design, the cost of which, happily, was covered by the insurance value of the stolen badge. The Masons (stolen in 1972) and the Apothecaries (stolen from the Hall on 24 February 1987) both had replicas made, the latter being commissioned from Garrards. The Woolmen (stolen in the 1960s) had a replacement badge donated by Past Master B.C. King.

The story of the Tallow Chandlers' badge is rather more of a mystery. The badge was stolen in 1963 and replaced with an exact replica. When this was cleaned and repaired in 2004 the jewellers found that the body of the badge was of Victorian construction and workmanship and it is considered possible that it might be the carcass of the original badge – though how this came about is open to conjecture.

Perhaps the most shattering theft is that reported in a history of the Butchers' Company:[1] 'Over the 1981 Easter Bank Holiday, thieves broke into Butchers' Hall

---

1   *A Cut Above the Rest* (2005).

through the kitchens. They went on to the strong room … and blew the door off the safe. It was a very professional raid … It was a devastating loss. The Court Regalia, the Master's Badge and chain, the Deputy Master's and the Renter Assistant's Badges and Clerk's all stolen …' Subsequently all were replaced by regalia created by Tessier.

Turning to lost badges that were eventually recovered, one can cite the Clockmakers, whose Master, in 1924, reported that he had left his badge on a bus on London Bridge. One would have liked to have been a fly on the wall at that particular Court meeting! He fined himself heavily and the insurers also paid out, so a new badge was commissioned. Then, in the 1960s the original was recovered and is now in the possession of the Clockmakers' Museum at Guildhall. Surprisingly, a gold replica of the new (1924 replacement) badge made in 1926 was also mislaid soon after its manufacture and yet was similarly recovered in 2003.

The Distillers' badge, an early example dating from 1852, was lost in the 1980s and a new badge, the work of Grant Macdonald was presented by Past Master Sichel. Subsequently, the original was found and the Court directed it should be used by the Immediate Past Master. However, in 2010 it was agreed to revert to the practice of its being the Master's Jewel.

The Tobacco Pipe Makers' Master's Badge, dating from 1952 when the Company was re-formed, was mislaid ten years later and, not being recovered, was replaced in 1962 with the current badge, the gift of their Master at that time.

Both the Mercers and the Fishmongers briefly believed they had lost their badges, the former when a Master declared he had left the badge in the back of a taxi; the latter when a Prime Warden reported his badge had gone missing. Happily both were recovered – presumably when one was returned by the cabbie and when the other was rediscovered in a sock drawer! Another story recounts that the Master Mariners had to pay a 'ransom' for the recovery of their badge after it fell from a window: colourful tales indeed![2]

War also took its toll, though in view of the devastation wrought by enemy action it is truly surprising that so few badges were lost or damaged. 'Most of the air raid damage to the City occurred on the nights December 29-30, 1940 and May 10-11, 1941. In these raids fifteen Halls were destroyed beside the two above-mentioned [the Merchant Taylors' on September 17, 1940 and the Mercers' on 11 May, 1941] and fifteen damaged; this is out of a total of thirty-five Halls. Since then, there has been so much further destruction and damage by the flying bomb, that very few Halls remain untouched.'[3] The Glovers, the Paviors, the Makers of Playing Cards and the Spectacle Makers lost their Master's Badges completely and the Cooks lost their Second Master's Badge,[4] whilst the Carmen's badge was damaged. Girdlers' Hall was destroyed in the blitz of December 1940 and the recovery of the badge is tensely recounted by the Master: 'On Wednesday, 1st January 1941 I went to Basinghall Street … and this time was permitted to enter the site of the Hall at my own risk. No words of mine can describe the horror and shock … when I realised that nothing but gaunt brick walls open to the sky remained … The next day we cut into the big strong room in the basement … [it] was like a glowing oven, it was indescribably hot, the smoke inside was choking and blinding and there was hot water to

---

2   Stories recounted to the author by Past Masters and Company officials – though none supported by written evidence.

3   *The Guilds of the City of London* (1945).

4   The Barbers lost their Middle Warden's Badge.

the depth of 12 inches or more … After two days' work we were able to find the head of the Mace, the Porter's wand and the badges of the Master and Wardens …'.[5]

As has already been mentioned, some Company regalia was commissioned to commemorate a notable event. So the Plumbers accepted the gift of a new badge for the Master in 1887 to commemorate Queen Victoria's Golden Jubilee. In the same year, and to commemorate the same Royal occasion, the Salters had a Master's Badge presented by Frederick Le Gros Clark and the Leathersellers were given a gold collar for the Master's Badge. The Cutlers' Master's chain, bearing the cypher VRI, was commissioned to commemorate Queen Victoria's Diamond Jubilee in 1897, as were the silver gilt badges for Wardens and Clerk that were provided for the Gardeners' Company.

An altogether more remarkable tale surrounded the new badge for the Master Clothworker. The badge, which replaced an earlier version, was designed in 1905 by John Bodman Carrington (who was married to a Clothworker Freewoman although he himself was Prime Warden of the Goldsmiths' Company 1903-4) and was intended to evoke the character of a 16th-century piece of jewellery. Three years earlier, Carrington had been commissioned to produce the crown to be worn by Queen Alexandra at the coronation of Edward VII, for it had been found that there was no suitable consort's crown in the regalia. The King, himself a Clothworker, agreed that after the ceremony the jewels would be retained by Carrington and he used the large diamonds for the Master's new badge which was presented by Court Assistant Frederick Morgan.[6]

In 1910 the Plaisterers gained a Master's chain to mark the occasion of the coronation of King George V.

Staying with royal connections, there is an apocryphal story that the pendant drop on the Painter-Stainers' badge was once an earring belonging to Queen Elizabeth I.

Moving from the regal to the civic, it should be mentioned that any number of badges are suspended from a clasp in the form of a shield of the arms of the City Corporation and that some of these include the full achievement with supporters and crest. Others show the City's shield beneath the main body of the badge and a few Companies have a depiction of the civic arms within the badge itself, as, for example, the Basketmakers, where their own shield of arms is sandwiched between those of the City and Middlesex. Both the Feltmakers and the Turners show their own shields side by side with those of the City Corporation.

Finally there are five companies where the Master's chain was at one time the shrieval chain of one of their liverymen who had served as Sheriff, these being the Apothecaries, Basketmakers, Clockworkers, Parish Clerks and Saddlers. The Firefighters also use a shrieval chain which was in the possession of the donor's family.

---

5 *The Girdlers' Company History.*
6 Correspondence from Jessica Collins, Archivist to the Clothworkers' Company.

IV

The Influence of Heraldry

The gentle art of heraldry had a far greater impact upon the replacement of badges than theft or war. The Bakers, for instance, had their first badge made by order of the Court in 1870. Now, the Bakers' Company corporate life was confirmed by Royal Charter dated 2 June 1486, though the fraternity was still divided into White and Brown Bakers and, whilst the joint guild received its first grant of arms in 1536 (confirmed when crest and supporters were added in 1590), the two branches still used distinct arms, those of the Whites known to exist *c*.1525 and the Browns who acquired their own grant in 1572. 'In 1645 the union of the bakers was effected by joint agreement and confirmed by Royal Charter of 1685.'[1] Unfortunately, the first Master's Badge made use of the Brown Bakers' arms not those of the united Company. So, in 1912 a new badge was commissioned bearing the accurate arms and was certificated by the College of Heralds as the correct version. Both badges are still available and seem to be worn at the Master's whim. Interesting the grant of arms included supporters (two bucks) but neither badge depicts these beasts.

Other companies have celebrated the augmentation of their arms with the creation of a new badge. The Bowyers, for instance, had supporters granted in 1996: one is a representation of a medieval bowyer in his Company's livery whilst the other is an archer of the time of Agincourt.[2] The full achievement now forms the new badge, itself also created in 1996.

The Upholders also had supporters, granted in 1963, and their Master commissioned and presented a new badge to commemorate the grant. However, this badge was itself superseded in 2000 when a new badge depicting the full achievement on a cushion was introduced. This was presented by the serving, and two Past, Masters and is inscribed with their names and the legend that it was to commemorate the Millennium.

Interestingly, the original Upholders' badge was one of only a very few that also depicted the shield of arms of the donor, in this case their Master, Edward Hunter.

---

1   *The Armorial Bearings of the Guilds of London* (1960).
2   Catalogue of Exhibition of the Bowyers' Company.

The Blacksmiths' badge also depicts a shield of arms, which presumably belonged to the Master or the donor although it has not been possible to confirm this, whilst the Furniture Makers' badge is engraved with the arms of the donor on the reverse.

The Carmen had no official arms when they decided to make a badge for their Master in 1893. The Court Minutes report that the arms chosen were those originally used by the Woodmongers with whom the Carmen had a bitter-sweet relationship in the 16th century. (Accused of corrupt charges for fuel, a 14 October 1667 bill to annul the Woodmongers' charter provoked its surrender on 5 December 1667.) The original arms were: 'Gules, a sword erect argent, hilt and pommel or, enfiled with a ducal coronet [or] between two flaunches argent charged with a faggot proper'. The use of unofficial arms was rectified by a Grant on 28 February 1929, when the principal charge, the sword, was retained although the faggots were replaced by more appropriate cart wheels. In 1938 the Company received a grant of supporters and this prompted the creation of a new badge

"The Arms and Crest of the Woodmongers Company of London (incorporating Fuellers and including Carmen) granted by Patent of Clarenceux King of Arms 1st October 1605, with Supporters, St. John the Baptist and St. Katherine, as used by the Company."

for the Master. Indeed, the Company's history relates that 'the rather grand arms required a rather grand badge … The new Master's Jewel cost £95 in gold and enamel in 1938'.[3]

It is fascinating to note that the Woodmongers' arms have also formed the basis of the shield granted to the Fuellers. After the demise of the Woodmongers, the interests of the coal trade were represented by The Society of Owners of Coal Craft (1739) and The Society of Coal Factors (1761). Then, in 1981, The Society of Coal Merchants reformed The Company of Woodmongers and Coal Sellers. Very quickly it was resolved to change the name to The Company of Fuellers and to petition for recognition as a City Company without Livery.

The Society of Coal Merchants had been granted arms that were based upon those once used by the Woodmongers. When the Fuellers received livery status in 1984 the arms granted, and shown on the Master's Badge, retained a shield that followed closely those used by both its predecessor organisations.

The Needlemakers had made use of unauthorised arms from at least 1680, with the background colour of the shield varying randomly from blue to green. This was addressed by the Company and when, in 1986, a grant of arms was received the shield was a definitive blue, although in all other respects the Kings of Arms accepted the traditional form of arms that had been used since the 17th century. A new badge was made at a cost of £2,200, raised through subscriptions from the Court of Assistants.

The Horners used arms that had no authority from at least the end of the 16th century and this shield was shown on their first badge of 1880 now used by the Deputy Master. Then in 1993 a formal Grant was received and, whilst this confirmed the original shield in an unchanged form, the crest that was granted was anything but traditional. It celebrated the association the Horners had developed with the plastics industry and more specifically the British Plastics Federation and included 'a representation of the Polyethylene Molecule' and 'a Ram … supporting between its forelegs a representation of the Benzene ring … enfiling … a Narwhal tusk'.[4] This remarkable Grant engendered an amazing new badge for the Master where the chemical symbols and the ram and narwhal tusk form the principal elements, with the shield added to one side. The design was the work of Sir David Hughes, Bt., who, from the 1960s, began experimenting with modeling small sculptures in wax, which he then had cast in solid metal. In 1979 he seized an opportunity to put this new interest on a business footing by buying the ailing firm of Louis Lejeune, producers of bronze and silver ornaments and car mascots.[5] Later he also developed a prominent specialty for himself: sculpting bespoke heraldic trophies and, of course, a Master's Badge for the Horners.

The Spectacle Makers' first badge for their Master was of unknown date, though probably mid-Victorian. It is thought to have depicted the 'pseudo-heraldic device' that the Company had adopted in 1810. This badge was lost by enemy action in the Blitz. In 1949 the Company opened negotiations with the College of Arms for an official Grant, which was made on 18 September 1950 and which prompted the commissioning of a replacement badge. The Heralds chose not to make use of the unofficial version but reverted to the earlier and simpler insignia that had been used from at least 1739. This second badge was itself supplanted by the manufacture of a new badge in 1991 and it is now used by the Deputy Master.

---

3   *Carr and Carmen* (1999).

4   From the official blazon of the Company's arms.

5   *Times* obituary.

The signatures include such luminaries of early aviation as Vernon Rowe, Sir Thomas Sopwith and Louis Bleriot himself. It was this design that formed the pattern for the Master's Badge which was presented to the Master by HRH The Duke of Kent at a Mansion House reception in 1936.

It is not uncommon for the College of Arms to grant arms that are distinctly different from those that had been previously unofficially adopted. This was the case with the Air Pilots and Air Navigators. When the Guild was first formed its original device was produced in about 1934 and has a genuine naivety in its conception. The early example shown above dates from a menu card of 25 July 1934, for a dinner at the Savoy held to commemorate the 25th Anniversary of Bleriot's cross-channel flight.

However, when the Air Pilots and Air Navigators applied for a formal grant of arms in September 1956 after the Guild obtained livery status in April of the same year, the Heralds eschewed the literal representation of an aeroplane and used the more symbolic image of two conjoined bird's wings, a simple roundel replaced the terrestrial globe and the charmingly direct motto 'We Fly' became the more dignified PER CAELUM VIA NOSTRA. New badges for many of the Guild's officers were later commissioned and these depict the official arms, but happily the original badge for the Master has been retained with its evocation of an earlier age of aviation.

Similarly, the Gunmakers used arms without authority from at least 1694 and the Master's Badge, made and presented by the Master himself in 1877, depicts the original device encompassed by an array of banners and weapons and other trophies of war. This was surrounded by a border of diamonds in 1884 and this badge is still in use despite the granting of authorised arms in 1973.

The Leathersellers had first been granted arms in 1479 but supporters were not added until 1505. Four hundred years later the arms were 'testified' by Garter King of Arms and in 1927 the Court Minutes record that H.S. Dove at his own expense had alterations made to the badge 'to make it heraldically correct'.

Much of the foregoing has of necessity discussed the heraldic aspects of the Companies' arms and their depiction on the badges. However, this work is not intended to be an heraldic treatise on the arms of the Livery for the very good reason that there already exists a quite excellent work that describes and explains the coats of arms of all City Companies up to the date of its publication. This is *The Armorial Bearings of the Guilds of London* by John Bromley and Heather Child (published by Frederick Warne & Co., 1960). However, since that date a further 28 Companies have achieved livery status and a number of already established Companies have received official grants of arms or augmentations to them. Accordingly, it has been thought helpful to offer an appendix giving the official blazon of the new Grants and, although the terminology may be strange to some, it should be easy enough to 'decode' the arcane language by reference to the illustration of the achievement of arms displayed.

So the review of the history and development of the Masters' Badges concludes and with it the trials and tribulations that have befallen so many of these jewels of the silversmiths' art. There now follows the photographs of each Company's badge together with a description and a detailed examination of its provenance. Not every Company has been able to provide complete information on its badges and, as mentioned elsewhere, it would be a delight to be able to fill in any missing data in a future edition.

PART II

The Worshipful Company of
MERCERS

DESCRIPTION OF MASTER'S BADGE
Within an ornate pierced foliate gold border inset with diamonds and rubies is set a light plain gold oval bearing the Company's shield of arms depicting a bust of a Maiden in coloured enamels, couped at the shoulders wearing a golden necklace with central ruby and a golden crown adorned with rubies and diamonds all on a background of red guilloche enamel and surrounded by a border of stylised clouds in blue enamel edged with white enamel and gold.

DATE OF MANUFACTURE AND DETAILS OF ANY HALLMARKS
1871 (no visible hallmarks)

NAME OF SILVERSMITH AND DESIGNER
G. Lambert of Coventry Street

SPECIAL REMARKS
On 21 April 1871 the Court resolved that a badge be provided at a cost not exceeding £100. It actually cost £125 and was the work of Lambert of Coventry Street. In 1936 the badge was altered when the inner enamelled badge was inserted in a light plain gold frame by Garrards following a design of Kruger Gray. In 1949 Garrards also made a miniature replica which was presented to Queen Mary on her admission to the Company. In the 1970s a Travelling Badge was commissioned (probably) the work of Hicklenton and Phillips. Thereafter the original badge was only to be worn within the Hall.

MASTER'S CHAIN
There is no chain. The badge is worn on a maroon (known as Mercers' red) neck ribbon.

OTHER BADGES
Other than the Master's Travelling Badge, there are no other badges

The Worshipful Company of
GROCERS

DESCRIPTION OF MASTER'S BADGE

Spices were used to construct the whole outside of the badge and included caraway and colunji, isal-gul, cumin, tukma and mustard. Several hundred of these were cast in 18ct red and yellow gold and assembled in a deep circular form, interspersed with diamonds to emphasise their preciousness. The outer form is circular but alters to a square shape at the inner edges. Contained within this squared shape is the complete coat of arms of the Company executed in red, yellow and white golds modelled three-dimensionally. The achievement is attached to the outer frame by fine round wires of yellow gold representing the mantling.

DATE OF MANUFACTURE AND DETAILS OF ANY HALLMARKS

1970

NAME OF SILVERSMITH AND DESIGNER

Designed and made by David Thomas

SPECIAL REMARKS

Historically the Master Grocer never wore a badge. This changed, following the destruction by fire of the fourth Grocers' Hall in 1965. To mark the opening of the fifth Hall in 1970 the other eleven of the Twelve Great Livery Companies commissioned a badge for the Master Grocer.

MASTER'S CHAIN

There is no chain. The badge is suspended on a simple green neck ribbon.

OTHER BADGES

There are no other badges

The Worshipful Company of
DRAPERS

DESCRIPTION OF MASTER'S BADGE

The jewelled badge is formed as an oval medallion, the centre set with an onyx cameo cut with the Company's Arms in high relief (the tiaras having diamond caps). The border is pierced and set with diamonds depicting the Company's motto 'UNTO GOD ONLY BE HONOUR AND GLORY'. The outer border is set with brilliants in open scrolls and leaf and ribbon ornament. A shimmering jewel.

DATE OF MANUFACTURE AND DETAILS OF ANY HALLMARKS

1882

NAME OF SILVERSMITH AND DESIGNER

Searle & Co., 1 Royal Exchange, London EC3

SPECIAL REMARKS

The back of the badge is of gold engraved 'Presented to the Drapers' Company by William Chapman, Esq. F.R.G.S. NOV 8th 1882 The first Court day after vacating the Chair as Master'.

MASTER'S CHAIN

There is no chain – the badge is worn on a blue ribbon

OTHER BADGES

4 Warden's Badges (1896) Maker: Searle & Co. donated by Past Master Frederick Harris

Past Master's Badges (1980) Maker: Asprey, donated by Martin Harris

Clerk's Badge in silver and enamel (1997) Maker: Martyn Pugh donated by Past Master Sir Michael Craig-Cooper, CBE

Court Assistants' Badges (2004). Maker: Gregor Anderson, donated by Past Master James Devereux

The Worshipful Company of
FISHMONGERS

DESCRIPTION OF PRIME WARDEN'S BADGE

A gold and enamelled oval badge showing the arms and crest of the Company with supporters and mantling, all modelled in high relief, beneath which is shown the Company motto in gold on a white enamel scroll. Decorated around the rim with scrollwork with fleur de lis at the bottom and entwined dolphins on the pendant attachment. The enamelling is of a particularly fine quality (measuring 57 x 111mm).

DATE OF MANUFACTURE AND DETAILS OF ANY HALLMARKS

1861 (Wood Badge) and 1877 ('Pretty' Badge)

NAME OF SILVERSMITH AND DESIGNER

J.S. & A.B. Wyon

SPECIAL REMARKS

The badge described above has engraved on the reverse 'John Samuel, Esq. Prime Warden 1877-8'. Known as the Samuel 'Pretty' Badge.

The 'Wood' Badge (not illustrated). The back is engraved 'Presented by Western Wood Esqr Prime Warden of the Fishmongers' Company 1861'. On an oval within a Garter border chased with the Company's motto is the achievement of the Company, the supporters and crest modelled in gold, the shield in various enamels. Worn by the Prime Warden with robes on special occasions such as Election Day. Date of manufacture, 1861.

PRIME WARDEN'S CHAIN

A double strand gold chain is worn with the Wood Badge

OTHER BADGES

The 'Shoobridge Badge'
The 'Gurney' Badge
5 Wardens Badges

The Worshipful Company of
GOLDSMITHS

DESCRIPTION OF PRIME WARDEN'S BADGE

An oval border set with diamonds within a double border of emeralds within which is depicted the arms of the Company in gold, with the red and blue quarters of the shield being composed of rubies and sapphires. The mantling and motto scroll shown in coloured enamels. All is pendant from a crowned lion's mask in gold.

DATE OF MANUFACTURE AND DETAILS OF ANY HALLMARKS

1953 (replacing the earlier original badge dating from 1948)

NAME OF SILVERSMITH AND DESIGNER

Designed by Donald Abbot and made by H.A. Byworth & Co. Ltd

SPECIAL REMARKS

The original badge was designed by Percy Metcalf and made by Leslie Durbin. It was to have been used as a 'Travelling Badge' when the current badge was commissioned in 1953 but has never been used for that purpose 'as it is considered too large and of dated appearance'.

PRIME WARDEN'S CHAIN

No chain. The badge is worn on a traditional red and white ribbon.

OTHER BADGES

The Prime Warden's Travelling Badge (1994) was designed and made by Lexi Dick
The Deputy Warden's Badge (1983) was designed by Alex Styles and made by Arthur Withers
3 Wardens Badges designed and made by John Donald (1959)
The Clerk's Badge (1981) was designed by Alex Styles and made by Naylor Bros. Ltd
(Together with others making a total of 10 official badges)

The Worshipful Company of
MERCHANT TAYLORS

DESCRIPTION OF MASTER'S BADGE

The full achievement of the Company's arms are modelled in three-dimensional pierced 18ct gold and enamel work within a foliate scroll frame and bead border attached with a Georgian gold and diamond ring, which forms the loop for the silk collar. The ring set with a central old cut diamond flanked with two bands of 33 diamonds set in a silver mount.

DATE OF MANUFACTURE AND DETAILS OF ANY HALLMARKS

1857-8
No hallmarks

NAME OF SILVERSMITH AND DESIGNER

Smith & Nicholson, Duke Street, Lincoln's Inn Field (whose name is engraved on the reverse)

SPECIAL REMARKS

There is a lengthy inscription on the reverse of the badge, giving the date 1857 making this one of the early badges. The scroll frame was added in 1873.

MASTER'S CHAIN

There is no chain

OTHER BADGES

An 18ct gold replica of the Master's Badge, worn by the Master when outside the City boundaries
Each of the four Wardens has a badge

The Worshipful Company of
SKINNERS

DESCRIPTION OF MASTER'S BADGE

Within two circles of gold encrusted with alternate diamonds and rubies and separated by gold leaves is set the full achievement of the Company's arms in gold and rich enamels. Beneath the motto is a gold domed circle edged in blue bearing the date 1327 in blue and white enamel with the roundel set at the edge with eight large diamonds set in gold.

DATE OF MANUFACTURE AND DETAILS OF ANY HALLMARKS

1874

NAME OF SILVERSMITH AND DESIGNER

SPECIAL REMARKS

The reverse of the badge is engraved with the names of the Master (Charles Barry) and four Wardens who had the badge made in 1874.

The date 1327 upon the badge is the date of the first Royal Charter granted to the Company by King Edward III.

MASTER'S CHAIN

There is no chain

OTHER BADGES

First Warden (gift of William Webb, Master 1883)
Second Warden (gift of L.B. Sebastian, Master 1894)
Third Warden (gift of G. Barton Kent, Master 1887)
Renter Warden (gift of L.B. Sebastian, Master 1894)

The Worshipful Company of
HABERDASHERS

DESCRIPTION OF MASTER'S BADGE

The badge depicts a jewelled representation of the Company's coat of arms set with emeralds, rubies, sapphires and diamonds. The lion passant is shown in raised yellow gold whilst the rampant goat supporters are in white gold set between two figures of St Catherine within a diamond-ruby-sapphire border with a jewelled enamel depiction of the motto 'Serve and Obey', above a surmount of the Company's crest of pink enamelled arms holding an emerald set wreath.

DATE OF MANUFACTURE AND DETAILS OF ANY HALLMARKS

1875
Gross weight 130 gms
3½" x 2½"

NAME OF SILVERSMITH AND DESIGNER

SPECIAL REMARKS

The reverse in inscribed: 'The Right Hon WJR Cotton Lord Mayor of London – MP and Senior Representative of the City Master. Provided by the Haberdashers' Company for the Master AD 1875.'

The depiction of St Catherine on the badge recalls that she was Patron Saint of the Company since the 14th century when Fraternity meetings were held in a side chapel dedicated to the saint in Old St Paul's Cathedral.

As the Company is now heavily involved in education, the coat of arms is to be seen on the uniforms of pupils of its 11 schools.

MASTER'S CHAIN

There is no chain

OTHER BADGES

Duplicate Master's Badge
Deputy Master's Badge
Immediate Past Master's Badge
4 Wardens Badges
Past Master's Badges
Mistress Brooch
Immediate Past Mistress Brooch
Past Mistress brooches (two styles)

The Worshipful Company of
SALTERS

DESCRIPTION OF MASTER'S BADGE

Within an ornate border of gold set with brilliant cut diamonds is a circle of gold beaded on the inner rim and containing an open lattice work of gold upon which is set the arms of the Company in gold and coloured enamels.

DATE OF MANUFACTURE AND DETAILS OF ANY HALLMARKS

1887
Hallmarked London (date letter Z) and 750

NAME OF SILVERSMITH AND DESIGNER

Messrs. Hunt & Roskell of 156 New Bond Street

SPECIAL REMARKS

The badge was presented by Frederick Le Gros Clark FRS in 1887 the year in which he was Master and to mark Queen Victoria's Golden Jubilee.

MASTER'S CHAIN

There is no chain

OTHER BADGES

Wardens
Past Masters

The Worshipful Company of
IRONMONGERS

DESCRIPTION OF MASTER'S BADGE
Within an ornate border of steel is set the full arms of the Company in pierced gold, silver and enamel work

DATE OF MANUFACTURE AND DETAILS OF ANY HALLMARKS
Presented to the Company in 1874

NAME OF SILVERSMITH AND DESIGNER
Hicklenton & Phillips
4¾" diameter

SPECIAL REMARKS
The use of steel in the construction of the Master's Badge is unique and very appropriate to the Ironmongers' Master's Badge

MASTER'S CHAIN

OTHER BADGES
Senior Warden's Badge by Hicklenton & Phillips (1882)
Junior Warden's Badge presented to the Company in 1882

The Worshipful Company of
VINTNERS

DESCRIPTION OF MASTER'S BADGE

18ct gold frame of enamelled grapes and vine leaves (enclosed by an outer rope border) surrounding a black onyx shield bearing the arms of the Company, with a diamond-set chevron and three silver tuns [barrels]. Beneath the shield is the Company's motto in gold on red enamel.
Dimensions: 10 cm x 6.2 cm.

DATE OF MANUFACTURE AND DETAILS OF ANY HALLMARKS

1878 replacing a badge of very early date [see below]

NAME OF SILVERSMITH AND DESIGNER

Made by Lambert & Co. of Coventry Street, London

SPECIAL REMARKS

Badge presented to the Company in 1878 by Frederick Barron, when in office as Master

MASTER'S CHAIN

18ct gold consisting of 14 chased beaded rope links, engraved on the reverse: 'Presented by Robert Berry, Master 1885'. Made by J. Avant of London c.1885.

OTHER BADGES

The Immediate Past Master's Badge is dated at c.1660-80 (although unmarked it can be dated stylistically to roughly the third quarter of the 17th century). It is therefore an extremely early example of a Master's Badge, always supposing that was its original function. It has been worn by the Immediate Past Master since 1930, but 'was probably originally the Master's Badge until supplanted in 1878 by Barron's gift.'
The Upper Warden's Badge dates from 1901 and was the gift of John Aste, Master
Master's Lady's Brooch 1962-3
Renter Warden (c.1901)
Court and Clerk (c.1880)

The Worshipful Company of
CLOTHWORKERS

DESCRIPTION OF MASTER'S BADGE

A sumptuous badge depicting the Company's arms in gold, with red, green, black and white enamels and diamonds used throughout to represent argent (silver) in the achievement including the helmet.

DATE OF MANUFACTURE AND DETAILS OF ANY HALLMARKS

1905 (replaces earlier badges of 1841 and 1872)

NAME OF SILVERSMITH AND DESIGNER

Designed by John Bodman Carrington, 'with a view of how to get the most definitive and simple effect of the character of a 16th-century jewel while preserving and adding to the symbolic and heraldic details thereof and enriching the same with the best stones and workmanship available.' The original – very early – badge dates from 1841 (now used by a Warden) was replaced in 1872 with a badge commissioned from Lambert & Co. This is now the Master's 'Travelling' Badge.

SPECIAL REMARKS

The badge was presented by Mr Frederick Morgan, Assistant. The large diamonds in the badge formed part of the crown worn at her coronation by Queen Alexandra in 1902. Her husband, King Edward VII, was a Clothworker. As no suitable consort's crown was available in the regalia a new crown was commissioned from Carrington on the understanding that he would retain the jewels afterwards.

MASTER'S CHAIN

There is no chain

OTHER BADGES

Master's Travelling Badge (see above)

Immediate Past Master (the work of John Donald and the gift of John Harding Jones, Master 2005/6)

4 Wardens' Badges (2 in gold and 2 in silver gilt – all cast by Benjamin Wyon and dating from 1841)

Clerk's Badge presented in 1961 by John E. Coomber, then Clerk to the Company

Past Master's Badge (one set purchased in 1961 from a legacy left by Henry Hawkins Turner, and a further set given by Eric Bousfield [Master, 1986/7])

The Worshipful Company of
DYERS

DESCRIPTION OF PRIME WARDEN'S BADGE

A white enamel shield upon which is painted the Company's arms, surmounted by the Company's crest in pierced gold and enamel work, all mounted on a gold wreath of laurels tied with a bow in green enamel. The whole suspended from an ornate gold bar to which is attached a dark red ribbon.

DATE OF MANUFACTURE AND DETAILS OF ANY HALLMARKS

*c.*1854

NAME OF SILVERSMITH AND DESIGNER

SPECIAL REMARKS

In 1854 the Court inaugurated gold medals for Past Prime Wardens. In 1901 the Court ordered that a special clasp be added to the Prime Warden's Gold Medal.

If the Prime Warden's Badge dates from 1854 it is one of the earliest on record

On the reverse is engraved 'The Prime Warden of the Dyers Company'

PRIME WARDEN'S CHAIN

There is no chain; the badge is suspended from a red ribbon

OTHER BADGES

Renter Warden's Badge – very similar to the Prime Warden's but suspended from a blue ribbon

Prime Warden's Lady's Badge

The Worshipful Company of
BREWERS

DESCRIPTION OF MASTER'S BADGE
The Company's shield of arms, motto and crest in silver gilt and enamel set within a decorative pierced frame in the 17th-century style. The charges are depicted in heavy relief whilst helm and crest are modelled in three dimensions.

DATE OF MANUFACTURE AND DETAILS OF ANY HALLMARKS
1900 Silver gilt and enamel

NAME OF SILVERSMITH AND DESIGNER

SPECIAL REMARKS
Presented to the Company in 1900 by William Thomas Paulin (Master in 1896). Court Minutes record: 'The Clerk reported that the Livery Dinner had been held at the Hall on 21st February and exhibited the badge presented by Mr William Thomas Paulin for the use of the Master on State occasions.' (8 March 1900).

MASTER'S CHAIN
There is no chain and the badge is worn on a blue ribbon

OTHER BADGES
There are badges for Past Masters and the Mistress Brewer has a brooch

The Worshipful Company of
LEATHERSELLERS

DESCRIPTION OF MASTER'S BADGE

The full achievement of the Company's arms is worked in gold, with the silvered shield emblazoned with red, blue and white enamel, the crest and mantling in red and white enamel with the motto at the base on a blue enamel scroll bordered with diamonds and beneath is set a cluster of diamonds forming a stylised fleur-de-lis.

DATE OF MANUFACTURE AND DETAILS OF ANY HALLMARKS

1934 (to replace original of 1871 that was reported lost in 1933)

NAME OF SILVERSMITH AND DESIGNER

The replacement was made by Harman & Lambert

SPECIAL REMARKS

In Oct 1871 the Court Minutes recorded that the first badge for the Master cost £120. In 1927 the Minutes record that H.S. Dove, at his own expense, had alterations made to the badge to make it heraldically correct. Perhaps this was a result of an official blazon being issued by Garter King of Arms in 1905.

In 1933 the Master reported that the badge had been stolen. A replica was ordered.

MASTER'S CHAIN

An ornate gold collar was given by J.D. Copeman (Master 1886-7) to mark Queen Victoria's Jubilee (1887). However, this has not been worn regularly since 1926 as it is somewhat fragile.

OTHER BADGES

3 identical Warden's Badges (1900) at a cost of 13 guineas
Immediate Past Master's Badge (1871)

TOTA·MEA·FIDUCIA·EST·IN·DEO

The Worshipful Company of
PEWTERERS

DESCRIPTION OF MASTER'S BADGE

On a shaped circle of gold decorated with foliage the coat of arms of the Company in heavy relief, the supporters modelled in silver gilt framing the shield in blue, red and green enamel and silver surmounted by a helm and crest in silver with mantling in blue enamel and beneath all the motto on a scroll.

DATE OF MANUFACTURE AND DETAILS OF ANY HALLMARKS

1871

NAME OF SILVERSMITH AND DESIGNER

George Lambert of Coventry Street

SPECIAL REMARKS

At a Court held on 25 May 1871 Past Master Mullins moved that a committee be appointed to consider the propriety of providing a suitable badge or medal for the Master to wear on State occasions. It was agreed that badges for the Master and Wardens be provided subject to the total cost not exceeding £20. Subsequently two designs for a Master's Badge were considered: one at £17.10.0, the other at £20. Accordingly the Wardens agreed to forego their badges and one for the Master was commissioned at £20. In October George Lambert wrote to say he could not 'work the badge as we intended' and asked for £22 – which was eventually agreed.

MASTER'S CHAIN

There is no chain

OTHER BADGES

Renter Warden
Upper Warden
Mistress Pewterer
Past Masters
Steward

The Worshipful Company of
BARBERS

DESCRIPTION OF MASTER'S BADGE

Silver, enamel and parcel gilt engraved with the Company's full armorial bearings within an open filigree quatrefoil shaped cartouche suspended from a crowned Tudor Rose clasp. The charges on the shield are in high relief and the supporters are worked in the round and elaborately enamelled and encircled by an outer ring of heavy beaded gold. The Company's motto is shown in gilt letters on a blue enamel scroll.

DATE OF MANUFACTURE AND DETAILS OF ANY HALLMARKS
Hallmarked London 1877

NAME OF SILVERSMITH AND DESIGNER
Lambert of Coventry Street
Charles John Shoppee

SPECIAL REMARKS

On 1 May 1877 it was resolved that a suitable Master's Badge with the Company's armorial bearings, supporters, crest and motto should be provided, enamelled in their proper colours, the estimated cost was 40 guineas. In June the design was presented at a cost of £44.9s.

The badge is engraved on the reverse: 'From Thomas Emerson, Frederick Wilson, Edward Raft, Charles Shoppee and Henley Grose Smith designed by Charles John Shoppee'. Charles Shoppee was Master Barber in 1878. He was also responsible for the design of a number of Master's Badges and was, indeed, Master of other Companies.

MASTER'S CHAIN

The triple link gold chain with enamelled side badge depicting the arms of the City of London was presented by Samuel George Shead, 22 September 1915. Weight approx 250 grams.

OTHER BADGES

Duplicate Master's Badge (The Travelling Badge) TKS Hallmarked London 1989
Silver gilt Warden's Badges (3) the gift of Sidney Michael Young (when Master in 1934)
The Middle Warden's Badge was destroyed in the Blitz in 1941 and replaced in 1941, the gift of Leonard Denny
A silver, gilt and enamel badge was given by John Carter (Master 1870) and this is now worn by the
    Deputy Master
Clerk's Badge (Grant Macdonald, London 1982)
Mistress's Badge (TKS 1989)
Past Masters also have badges and there are badges for Hon. Librarian, Hon. Curator, Hon. Chaplain,
    Hon. Information Technology Adviser, Hon. Curator of the Physic Garden and Archivist (all Grant
    Macdonald 1998)

The Worshipful Company of
CUTLERS

DESCRIPTION OF MASTER'S BADGE

Pierced gold and enamel emblazoned arms of the Company with a shield of the City arms below and a loop of diamonds for attachment to the collar above.

DATE OF MANUFACTURE AND DETAILS OF ANY HALLMARKS

1880

NAME OF SILVERSMITH AND DESIGNER

SPECIAL REMARKS

The badge was provided by the Court and is inscribed on the reverse 'The Worshipful Company of Cutlers. W.A. Oldaker, Master. A. Pocock, J.P. Edkins, Wardens AD 1880'.

MASTER'S CHAIN

A gold chain with central monogram in enamel 'V.R.I.' surmounted with a crown and the date 1897. The chain contains 26 links of 'C.C.' alternating with 23 shields for the names of Masters and 2 shields bearing the arms of the Company in enamel.

OTHER BADGES

Wardens
Court Assistants
Past Masters have a bar on the ribbon of their Court badge
Clerk
Master's Lady
Stewards

The Worshipful Company of
BAKERS

DESCRIPTION OF MASTER'S BADGES

1) The shield of arms (of the Brown Bakers) in gold and enamel is set into a golden oval bearing the Company's motto within a decorated border. To top, bottom, left and right of the border are set four semi-precious stones (cabochon and brown/white agates). The badge is surmounted by a golden wheat sheaf.

2) On a gold oval inset with white enamel is a painted representation of the shield surmounted by the crest of the Company all set within an elaborate filigree border incorporating the motto on a scroll of white enamel in base and a gold wheat sheaf above.

DATE OF MANUFACTURE AND DETAILS OF ANY HALLMARKS

1) Hallmarked 22ct gold, London 1875 J.B.

2) Hallmarked 18ct gold J.W. & T, London 1912

SPECIAL REMARKS

In 1870 the Great Badge for the Master and the smaller badges for the Court were made by order of the Court. The arms were not shown correctly as they depicted those of the 'Brown Bakers'. Indeed, the reverse is engraved 'The badge of the Worshipful Company of Brown Bakers, made by order of the Court February 1876, Alex Whitten, Esq., Master'. In July 1912 the Master (W.T. Roberts) presented a new badge 'being a correct copy of the arms of the Company as certified by the Heralds' Office'. Both badges are still in use with the Master choosing which he wishes to wear.

MASTER'S CHAIN

9ct gold chain incorporating a 'handsome' enamelled panel centre link depicting the armorial bearings and motto of the Bakers' Company together with 14 links pierced and enamelled with wheat sheaves and scales on a woven back chain, with reverse inscription: 'Presented to the Worshipful Company of Bakers by H M Joseph CBE, Master 1984/85 in celebration of the 500th Anniversary'. Hallmarked 9ct by Thomas Fattorini, Birmingham 1985.

OTHER BADGES

Wardens and Clerk.

Court Assistants receive a silver badge on appointment. This is relinquished on appointment as a Warden and returned when they become Past Masters when it is embellished by an outer enamelled ring.

The Worshipful Company of
WAX CHANDLERS

DESCRIPTION OF MASTER'S BADGE

The Company's full achievement of arms in pierced gold, silver gilt and blue and red enamelwork. The mantling elaborately pierced and filling the space around the achievement. All set within a decorated square golden frame, and at each corner a roundel bearing the monogram WCWC, all suspended by two chains from a golden beehive.

DATE OF MANUFACTURE AND DETAILS OF ANY HALLMARKS

Victorian

NAME OF SILVERSMITH AND DESIGNER

SPECIAL REMARKS

Commissioned by the Court

MASTER'S CHAIN

Presented by a Past Master in 2002

OTHER BADGES

Upper Warden ⎫ Similar design
Renter Warden ⎬ to Master's
Deputy Master ⎭ Badge
Past Masters
Clerk – donated by a previous Clerk in 1991

The Worshipful Company of
TALLOW CHANDLERS

DESCRIPTION OF MASTER'S BADGE
The full achievement of the Company's arms including the two crests (on the two helms which are shown facing one another) are depicted in 22ct yellow gold, platinum and enamels and set with 111 diamonds. All aspects of the design modelled in three dimensions and of the finest quality enamels. The symbols on the badge are entirely religious in allusion, reflecting the Company's origin as a religious fraternity.

DATE OF MANUFACTURE AND DETAILS OF ANY HALLMARKS
1963 (The original of 1883/4 stolen in 1963)

NAME OF SILVERSMITH AND DESIGNER
The new badge was made by Hicklenton & Phillips in 1963 measuring 12.5 cm by 8.5cm

SPECIAL REMARKS
Robert John Kell (Master 1883 and 1886) presented the first Master's Badge in 1883/4. Later he offered to add the diamonds, which cost in excess of £200. This badge was stolen in 1963 and replaced with a replica. When this was repaired and cleaned in 2004 the jewellers found that the body of the badge was of Victorian construction and workmanship and it is considered it might be the carcass of the original badge.

MASTER'S CHAIN
There is no chain. The Master's Badge is worn on a ribbon on which is embroidered three doves.

OTHER BADGES
Master's Travelling Badge
Wardens
Clerk
Past Masters' Badges
Bargemaster
Court Assistants
Wine Waiters

The Worshipful Company of
ARMOURERS AND BRASIERS

DESCRIPTION OF MASTER'S BADGE

Within an elaborately chased gold square frame with arched sides are set, in pierced work, the two shields of the Company in gold and enamel surmounted by the helm and crest in gold, platinum and enamel within the Company's supporters worked in the round and encircled with decorative mantling in gold. The two mottoes are shown one above and one beneath the shields in gold lettering on blue enamel. At the base of the badge is the shield of the City in gold and enamel work.

DATE OF MANUFACTURE AND DETAILS OF ANY HALLMARKS

1875

NAME OF SILVERSMITH AND DESIGNER

Lambert of Coventry Street.

The work was overseen by Charles Shoppee who was Master Armourer & Brasier in 1877-8 and 1896. He was also responsible for the design of a number of other Master's Badges and was, indeed, Master of other Companies.

SPECIAL REMARKS

A recent history records: 'The increased revenue and perhaps too a certain rise in self-awareness caused by the public attacks [on the Livery] had other effects and in 1875 the company commissioned a splendid Master's Badge.' Elsewhere it is reported that the badge was the gift of Charles Wood (Master 1874).

MASTER'S CHAIN

The Master's chain is gold with enamel shields and is dated 1878. It was gifted to the Company by Edward Baddeley (Master 1888).

OTHER BADGES

Upper Warden's Badge and chain in gold, badge the gift of Charles Hale (Master 1882). The chain was the gift of Henry Pontifex (Assistant) in 1878.

The Renter Warden's Badge is gold and enamel and was the gift of Charles Tyler (Upper Warden) in 1886. Its chain is also gold.

There are also badges for the Immediate Past Master, the Father of the Company and the Chairman of Trustees of the Company's charity. Past Masters have badges with gold chains, whilst Assistants below the Chair have badges with ribbons. The Master's and the Upper Warden's ladies have brooches.

The Worshipful Company of
GIRDLERS

DESCRIPTION OF MASTER'S BADGE

The badge is cast and pierced in 18ct gold with an enamelled coat of arms set with sapphires and rubies. Around the achievement are set designs depicting notable features from the Company's history.

DATE OF MANUFACTURE AND DETAILS OF ANY HALLMARKS

1950 (replacing original of 1880)
The badge is Hallmarked D.S.& G, London 18ct

NAME OF SILVERSMITH AND DESIGNER

Gowland Brothers Ltd., Cornhill, London

SPECIAL REMARKS

On the reverse is engraved: 'Presented to the Worshipful Company of Girdlers by Lionel C. Straker CC Master 1940-41 on the 14th December 1950'. It replaced the original badge that had been presented by Judge Philbrick on the termination of his year of office in 1880. This is now used by the Immediate Past Master. This badge was rescued from the basement strong room of the Hall after its destruction in the blitz of 1940.

There is a Travelling Badge in silver gilt for use by the Master which is the work of Grant Macdonald (London 2007) and the gift of Sir Charles Burnett, Bt. (Master 2006-7).

MASTER'S CHAIN

48 inches long, the chain comprises 30 links (cast as gridirons) in gold and was the gift of Past Master David James (1997-8) and was made by R.A. Jones of London.

OTHER BADGES

Morrison Fairclough, another Past Master, has presented smaller badges of the same character (to the Master's) for the three wardens.

A Lady's Badge was given by Past Master Sir Michael Newton and a second Lady's Badge was given in 2002 by Past Master Martin French.

The Worshipful Company of
BUTCHERS

DESCRIPTION OF MASTER'S BADGE

A very fine and spirited rendition of the full achievement of the Company's arms in 18ct yellow gold and various coloured enamels. Much of the design is in heavy relief and the supporters, etc are depicted in the round.

DATE OF MANUFACTURE AND DETAILS OF ANY HALLMARKS

1986 (replacing original of 1874 which was itself replaced in 1978)

NAME OF SILVERSMITH AND DESIGNER

Robin and Phillipa Kyte

SPECIAL REMARKS

The badge and chain were presented by Past Master Norman Poultney following a major theft from Butchers' Hall in 1982.

The original was presented by Benjamin Venables in 1874 and a chain comprising 8 oval plaques, the arms of the City and the Butchers' Company alternate in gold and enamel and 8 monograms (BG) together with an enamel plaque of Smithfield Market was presented by John Gardner in 1919.

MASTER'S CHAIN

Gold chain made by Jocelyn Burton (1986) with 18 sapphires, 4 bull's heads and 4 ram's heads with the Company's arms on the rear plate and the City arms on the front plate. It replaced that stolen in 1982.

OTHER BADGES

A Master's 'Day' Badge in 9ct gold, the arms in pink enamels in full relief and supporters with rubies was made by Tessiers in 1982

A Lady Master's Badge, being a 'Day' Badge first used by HRH The Princess Royal in her year as Master (2010-11)

Deputy Master's Badge

Clerk

Renter Assistant

The Worshipful Company of
SADDLERS

DESCRIPTION OF MASTER'S BADGE

Within a gold scroll border decorated with saddles linked by reins and inset with sapphires is set a cast appliqué silver and gold and coloured enamel coat of arms of the Company mounted on a matt finished plate with a polished oval removable back plate.

The badge measures 2½" by 3" and is of 18ct gold and enamel.

DATE OF MANUFACTURE AND DETAILS OF ANY HALLMARKS

1868

NAME OF SILVERSMITH AND DESIGNER

SPECIAL REMARKS

The removable back plate is engraved 'The badge of the Master of the Worshipful Company of Saddlers, the only existing Anglo Saxon Guild. 1868'.

MASTER'S CHAIN

Three rows of gold chain links and below a gold and enamel shield bearing the arms of the City. This was originally the Shrieval chain of Deputy H.W.S. Horlock, Master 1976 and Sheriff in 1978 and was given by him to the Company in 1989.

OTHER BADGES

The Wardens' and Clerk's Badges by C.J. Vander Ltd., London 1964
Chaplain's Badge by Christopher Lawrence, London 1994

HONOUR GOD

1333 — 1933

The Worshipful Company of
CARPENTERS

DESCRIPTION OF MASTER'S BADGE

In 18ct gold in the Art Deco style, two standing naked winged female figures support the shield of arms of the Company, the charges shown in black enamel on a silvered shield. This is held aloft by a kneeling cherub who also supports a banner engraved '1333-1933 Honour God' It is set with diamonds being held by two more cherubs and set with six sapphires and a moonstone.

DATE OF MANUFACTURE AND DETAILS OF ANY HALLMARKS

1933 to commemorate the 600th anniversary of the Company and replacing the original of 1871

NAME OF SILVERSMITH AND DESIGNER

The badge is stamped 'Fecit me arle et opera sua Omar Ramsden'

SPECIAL REMARKS

On the reverse is engraved 'I was wrought for the Worshipful Company of Carpenters to commemorate the 600th Year of the making of the Boke of Ordinances in 1333 and delivered into the keeping of the Master by His Royal Highness Edward Prince of Wales at a banquet on March 22nd 1933.'

Interestingly, the Company has no grant of supporters but frequently made use of two naked boys or cherubs, which the designer has here changed to elegant women.

MASTER'S CHAIN

A fourfold gold chain presented by Mr Jowers

OTHER BADGES

The original Master's Badge is now used as the Master's Travelling Badge and was ordered in 1871 for £67
3 Wardens' Badges in 18ct gold dated 1875 and presented by Mr Faulconer

The Worshipful Company of
CORDWAINERS

DESCRIPTION OF MASTER'S BADGE
The Company's arms in 18ct gold and blue and white enamel set within a golden border which is itself enclosed in a (later) further ornamental border of gold including two winged beasts and decorated with pearls and diamonds.

DATE OF MANUFACTURE AND DETAILS OF ANY HALLMARKS
Original inner badge 1891
Border of seed pearls and diamonds added in 1921

NAME OF SILVERSMITH AND DESIGNER

SPECIAL REMARKS
Presented by Frederick Clarke and inscribed on the reverse 'Frederick Clarke, Master 1891'.
The outer ring of seed pearls and diamonds was the gift of Augustus Hughes-Hughes (Master 1921).
The reverse is engraved 1891 with the names of the Master and four Wardens.

MASTER'S CHAIN
There is a chain

OTHER BADGES
Wardens (2)
Chaplain
Clerk
Past Masters
Bargemaster – now worn by the Company's Beadle

The Worshipful Company of
PAINTER-STAINERS

DESCRIPTION OF MASTER'S BADGE

Composed of a large circular plaque with inward scrolls and blue enamel background, each alternate scroll set with a cushion shaped old cut brilliant diamond (4) and one round brilliant, the raised circular centre plaque (48mm diameter) within a green enamelled border set at quarter points with a collet set oval red cabochon garnet. Around a centre plaque is embossed 'The Worshipful Company of Painters' 'Amor Et Obedientia' within which is set the full achievement of the Company's arms. Beneath the plaque is a pendant drop composed of a pear-shaped clear quartz polished crystal within a gold open frame.

DATE OF MANUFACTURE AND DETAILS OF ANY HALLMARKS

1881
Gross weight 300 gms; 147mm x 84mm

NAME OF SILVERSMITH AND DESIGNER

John Gregory Crace

SPECIAL REMARKS

Reverse bears the inscription: 'Presented to the Painters Company by George Mence-Smith Liveryman 5th October 1881. Designed by John Gregory Crace, Esq. Past Master and presented on the occasion of the installation of Wilfred Nicholson, Esq. as Master 18th October 1881.'

MASTER'S CHAIN

Composed of scrolled linked chain with alternate plaques of a Phoenix on a blue enamel background and an enamelled rose. Hallmarked silver-gilt inscribed on reverse 'Presented to the Painters Company by Hunter Donaldson, Master 1898'. 88cm long.

OTHER BADGES

Upper Warden and Renter Warden's Badges both inscribed: 'Commissioned to commemorate the Quincentenary of the Granting of Arms. Presented by the Master Gordon A. Luton 1986.' Hallmarked TKS Birmingham. Each with a chain of office presented by J.C. Nicholson, Upper Warden 1912-13
Past Masters
Clerk
Honorary Chaplain
Honorary Archivist

The Worshipful Company of
CURRIERS

DESCRIPTION OF MASTER'S BADGE

In 18ct yellow gold, rose gold and platinum and enamel the badge shows the Company's arms surmounting a shield of the City arms and all set within a decorative gold border set with 24 natural oriental pearls and 7 rubies.

Dimensions: 4" x 3½"

DATE OF MANUFACTURE AND DETAILS OF ANY HALLMARKS

1884

NAME OF SILVERSMITH AND DESIGNER

Designed by John Belcher

Made by Lambert & Co. of Coventry Street

SPECIAL REMARKS

The reverse is engraved '1884 Presented to the Worshipful Company of Curriers by Emma Burkitt'. This was done in memory of her brother, Edward Burkitt, the Clerk of the Company from 1833 to 1881.

John Belcher, the designer, was an architect who was renowned for designing both the V&A Museum and the Institute of Chartered Accountants. He became Master Currier in 1886.

MASTER'S CHAIN

Silver gilt with hallmarks for London 1993, makers Ross V Turner, presented to the Company by Michael Chesterton (Master 1991), Malcolm Simmonds (Master 1992) and Sir Frank Sanderson (Master 1993) comprising 29 links enclosing the crossed shaving knives from the Company's arms.

OTHER BADGES

9ct gold Clerk's Badge (Presented in 1955 by Past Master Robert Robertson)

3 silver gilt badges of the Upper and Renter Wardens and the Father of the Company, all London 1873. Maker's mark: 'R.C.' Junior Warden's Badge (London 1964 presented by Leslie Minty, Master 1963-4)

The Worshipful Company of
MASONS

DESCRIPTION OF MASTER'S BADGE
On a gold oval set within a border of 9ct gold loops is depicted the Company's shield, helm, crest and motto in silver and gold and black, white, blue, pink and green enamel.

DATE OF MANUFACTURE AND DETAILS OF ANY HALLMARKS
1973 (replaces 1873 original)

NAME OF SILVERSMITH AND DESIGNER
Hicklenton & Phillips

SPECIAL REMARKS
In 1873 it was resolved by the Court that some suitable badge or insignia should be provided for the Master
This badge was stolen in December 1972 and the present replacement commissioned

MASTER'S CHAIN
A 9ct gold three-strand chain with hook and pins

OTHER BADGES
2 Wardens' Badges in gold, 1881
Master's Lady Badge with chain
Clerk, 1982
20 Past Master's Badges, 1963
Master's Lady miniature Badge (1977)
Chaplain's Badge

The Worshipful Company of
PLUMBERS

DESCRIPTION OF MASTER'S BADGE

The full achievement of the Company's arms is depicted in brightly burnished gold with the charges on the shield depicted in raised silver, blue and black enamels, the helm in gold and blue enamel surmounted by the crest in gold and coloured enamels. Beneath is a scroll of gold with white enamel and the motto in black letters.

DATE OF MANUFACTURE AND DETAILS OF ANY HALLMARKS

1887 (replacing original of 1876)
The badge was reconditioned in 1994

NAME OF SILVERSMITH AND DESIGNER

SPECIAL REMARKS

On 29 June 1876 the sum of £25 was paid to Vince Bensson & Co. for the Master's Badge. In June 1887 Alderman Sir Stuart Knill, Bt (Master and later Lord Mayor) presented to the Company a new jewel to be worn by the Master during his term … the old jewel was to be worn by the Immediate Past Master – the whereabouts of this badge is not now known. The reverse bears the following inscriptions.

Reconditioned Queen Elizabeth II 1994 George E. Bank Master.

Ye Companie of Plumbers.
ORDINANCES EDWARD III 1381
GRANT OF ARMS Elizabeth 1588
CHARTER James 1612
This jewel was given VICTORIA 1887
By ALDERMAN STUART KNILL Master in this Jubilee Year.

In 1728 Coronets (garlands) were recorded in the inventory.

MASTER'S CHAIN

A chain comprising roundels on a fabric collar

OTHER BADGES

Wardens

The Worshipful Company of
INNHOLDERS

DESCRIPTION OF MASTER'S BADGE

On a gold oval with an elaborate raised border including grapes and vine leaves and set with four amethysts is a raised depiction of the Company's achievement of arms in gold and enamel.

DATE OF MANUFACTURE AND DETAILS OF ANY HALLMARKS

1879 (remade 1929)
Gross weight 210 gm stamped 18ct
Overall dimensions 95mm x 80mm

NAME OF SILVERSMITH AND DESIGNER

SPECIAL REMARKS

On the reverse is engraved 'This Master's Badge of the Worshipful Company of Innholders was presented February 1879 Mr William Nathan, Master re-designed and remade 1929 Mr H. Edmund Mathews OBE HML Master'.

It should be noted (see below) that the Middle Warden's Badge dates from the 1780s and could well have been used by the Master prior to 1879. It has the appearance of an early livery badge.

MASTER'S CHAIN

There is no chain

OTHER BADGES

Middle Warden (hallmarked 1784) and a gift of J. Pearson (Master 1789)
Renter Warden 1914
Upper Warden 1895
Clerk 1950
Master's Wife 1976

The Worshipful Company of
FOUNDERS

DESCRIPTION OF MASTER'S BADGE
The Company's shield in silver bordered blue enamel with the charges moulded in heavy relief in silver – beneath is the motto in silver on a blue enamel scroll and above the shield a silver helm with the crest in silver and orange enamel and mantling cascading around the shield in white and red enamels.

DATE OF MANUFACTURE AND DETAILS OF ANY HALLMARKS
Indistinct hallmarks (perhaps 1924)

NAME OF SILVERSMITH AND DESIGNER
Spencer of London

SPECIAL REMARKS
The reverse is engraved 'THE WORSHIPFUL COMPANY OF FOUNDERS¦FOUNDERS HALL¦ST SWITHINS LANE EC4¦MASTER'S BADGE'

MASTER'S CHAIN
The chain is silver gilt and enamelled with flat pierced links. Birmingham hallmark 1924

OTHER BADGES
2 early Wardens' Badges (plain and early Edwardian)
2 later Wardens' Badges – silver gilt and enamelled 1963-4
Clerk's Badge in silver gilt (1963-4)
Past Master's Badges

The Worshipful Company of
POULTERS

DESCRIPTION OF MASTER'S BADGE

Set on an open oval border of gold and blue enamel is a spirited rendition of the Company's full achievement of arms in gold and coloured enamels. All pendant from the full coat of arms of the City in gold and coloured enamels.

DATE OF MANUFACTURE AND DETAILS OF ANY HALLMARKS

1879

NAME OF SILVERSMITH AND DESIGNER

SPECIAL REMARKS

On the reverse of the badge is inscribed: PRESENTED TO THE WORSHIPFUL COMPANY OF POULTERS LONDON BY SIR CHAS. D. CROSLEY MASTER 1878

MASTER'S CHAIN

The Master's collar in silver gilt was the gift of W.C. Parsons (1900)

OTHER BADGES

Wardens
Clerk
Past Masters
Beadle

The Worshipful Company of
COOKS

DESCRIPTION OF MASTER'S BADGE

Silver gilt representation of the Company's arms being shown in high relief with the shield enamelled in colour. The ornamental background consists of acanthus leaves in pierced work.

DATE OF MANUFACTURE AND DETAILS OF ANY HALLMARKS

1872

NAME OF SILVERSMITH AND DESIGNER

SPECIAL REMARKS

The badge was prepared by an Order of the Court in 1872. A century earlier the Court authorised the livery to have medals (1772).

The chevron in the arms is shown as red rather than the correct black – which was a variation introduced in the middle of the 18th century, although the Company has now reverted to the correct colour in representation of its arms.

The Company still crowns its Officers, new velvet crowns having recently replaced the Victorian versions.

As the Company has a Second Master there is also a badge for this office (see below).

MASTER'S CHAIN

A gold 'curb' chain was presented by Robert Miller in 1881

OTHER BADGES

The Second Master's Badge was presented in 1879 by John Phillips but was lost in enemy action in 1940 and subsequently replaced in 1948/49 and is hallmarked and engraved 'Worshipful Company of Cooks 2nd Master's Badge Presented by B.B. Tarring, Master 1948-49'

Warder's Badge presented in 1879 by Robert Miller, subsequently lost and replaced

Renter Warden's Badge presented in 1878 by Robert Miller, subsequently lost and replaced

Immediate Past Master's (called the Last Master) Badge presented in 1910 by Alfred Charles Goodinge

Father of the Company's Badge presented in 2000 by bequest from Harry Tickler

Clerk's Badge presented in 1966 by G. Swan

The Worshipful Company of
COOPERS

DESCRIPTION OF MASTER'S BADGE
A fine and weighty representation of the Company's achievement is shown in gold and various coloured enamels with the motto 'Love as Brethren' entwined around the supporters.

DATE OF MANUFACTURE AND DETAILS OF ANY HALLMARKS
1872

NAME OF SILVERSMITH AND DESIGNER

SPECIAL REMARKS
Presented in 1872 by the Immediate Past Master, Mr Thomas Rowland Legg

MASTER'S CHAIN
Silver gilt chain of open-work links presented in 1903/04 by Andrew J. Chalmers (Master 1903-4)

OTHER BADGES
3 gold Warden's Badges donated in 1873 by the Master, Mr Cyrus Legg
Clerk's Badge (1966) in silver gilt and enamel
Court Assistants receive a silver badge on election which is gilded when the owner passes the chair

The Worshipful Company of
TYLERS AND BRICKLAYERS

DESCRIPTION OF MASTER'S BADGE

A silver gilt circle with a border of balls within which is set a scalloped frame in the form of a six-petal foil, part pierced within which is a silver-edged shield of blue enamel and the charges modelled in raised silver and silver gilt beneath which is the motto in silver on blue enamel. Above is a silver helm and the Company's crest in coloured enamels the upraised arm holding a brick axe traversing the outer border and to which is attached a hook for the collar. The shield is surrounded by the mantling in red and silver enamel.

DATE OF MANUFACTURE AND DETAILS OF ANY HALLMARKS

*c.*1890

NAME OF SILVERSMITH AND DESIGNER

SPECIAL REMARKS

Engraved on the reverse 'Presented to the Company by Stanley George Bird' (who served on the Court from 1882 to 1892) probably donated *c.*1890.

Earlier, in 1876 the Court re-introduced the wearing of robes for Court Meetings at a cost of some £40 to £50.

Silver medals for Liverymen were introduced in 1772 at 12/6 each with the owner paying 5/-.

MASTER'S CHAIN

Master's chain dates from 1978. It is a long 28-section necklace of alternate oval links and wheat sheaves in silver gilt. Maker's mark is DAT, dated London 1978. There is an earlier gold chain that was used from 1870 to 1976 comprised of 97 shields, on which was engraved all the Masters' names. It was replaced when all the available space (on 97 shields) was used up.

OTHER BADGES

Badges for the Wardens
Clerk's Badge gift of PM Jeremy Stokes in 1999
Past Masters' Badges (dating from 1906/7)
Father of the Company has a badge, or rather a locket presented to the Company in 1865 and known as the
    Mansfield Locket after the donor

The Worshipful Company of
BOWYERS

DESCRIPTION OF MASTER'S BADGE

The full achievement of the Company's arms, including supporters, shown in coloured enamels upon a silver gilt oval, surrounded by a decorated open border. The title 'Master' and 'Worshipful Company of Bowyers' is shown in gilt letters on black enamel to the top and bottom respectively of the achievement.

DATE OF MANUFACTURE AND DETAILS OF ANY HALLMARKS

1996 (replacing original of 1884)
Hallmarked

NAME OF SILVERSMITH AND DESIGNER

Silver gilt by Fattorini, Birmingham

SPECIAL REMARKS

The 1884 original, manufactured by Lamberts of Coventry Street and now worn by the Immediate Past Master, was replaced in 1996 when the Company was granted supporters by the College of Arms. 'Poitiers' is wrongly shown as 'Poiters'.

MASTER'S CHAIN

Master's collar, alternate panels of cut-cornered rectangles with *flote* (an iron tool for shaping a bow) motif and plain ovals with attached scroll work all connected with chain. Silver gilt by Toye, Kenning & Spencer, Birmingham 1980.

OTHER BADGES

Immediate Past Master (previously the Master's Badge)
Master's Lady's Brooch (2002)
Wardens' Badges (1884 Lambert))
Past Masters' Badges (earliest from 1884 Lambert)
Court Assistants
Clerk (1980 Toye, Kenning)

The Worshipful Company of
FLETCHERS

DESCRIPTION OF MASTER'S BADGE

On a silver oval set around the rim with small balls is an oval of light blue enamel upon which is displayed an ornate shield of the Company's arms in silver and black enamel surmounted by the helmet, crest and mantling and beneath the Company motto all in silver and enamel. The oval is supported by two upright cornucopia upon which are set two demi-maidens one holding a bow and an arrow and the other a trumpet. Beneath all, a small shield engraved with a man's (or satyr's) mask and set on either side with quivers containing arrows.

DATE OF MANUFACTURE AND DETAILS OF ANY HALLMARKS

1899 (replacing original of 1879)
Hallmarked London and Lion Passant and maker's mark G.K.
No date letter

NAME OF SILVERSMITH AND DESIGNER

George Kenning & Son from a design submitted to the Court by Mr J. Thomas

SPECIAL REMARKS

On 10 June 1879 the Master, Mr Brock Hunt, produced a handsome silver gilt medal which he had struck, appended to an appropriate ribbon.

This badge is now worn by the Renter Warden when the Master's Badge was superseded by the present badge in 1899 to a design by Mr J. Thomas. Its costs were borne by a contribution of two guineas from each member of the Court supplemented by £25 from Company funds.

MASTER'S CHAIN

Gold plated discs (19th-century)

OTHER BADGES

Upper Warden (original *c*.1923)
Renter Warden (original Master's Badge)
Junior Warden (originally Renter Warden's Badge, presented by W. Brock Hunt)
Clerk
Past Masters (from 1928)
Stewards

The Worshipful Company of
BLACKSMITHS

DESCRIPTION OF PRIME WARDEN'S BADGE

The Company's shield of arms in enamel, 18ct yellow gold and silver and the motto (gold lettering on white enamel) is set upon a gold disc intricately pierced to show blue enamel beneath. This is surmounted by a silver helm on which sits a rising phoenix in gold. All is set within an elaborate heavy golden frame in Victorian Gothic style at the base of which is another shield and motto and beneath which is suspended a golden acorn.

DATE OF MANUFACTURE AND DETAILS OF ANY HALLMARKS

1870
Weight over 100 grams

NAME OF SILVERSMITH AND DESIGNER

SPECIAL REMARKS

The chevron in the arms is shown in red enamel when it should be gold.

The reverse is engraved 'Presented to the Worshipful Company of Blacksmiths by James Abbiss, Esq., JP July 7th 1870 J.G. Nicoll, Esq Prime Warden'.

The small shield might well refer to the donor although the motto shown 'PAX QUAERITUR BELLO' and the arms cannot be traced to either family name.

PRIME WARDEN'S CHAIN

18ct gold chain presented by Past Prime Warden Charles Ravenhill in 1870

OTHER BADGES

Renter Warden and 4th Warden's Badges, presented in 1937 by Alfred Barrow
'Indian Necklace' for use of Prime Warden's Lady presented in 1941/3
Father of the Company's Badge presented in 1966

The Worshipful Company of
JOINERS AND CEILERS

DESCRIPTION OF MASTER'S BADGE
Within an elaborate heavily chased silver circular border, at the top of which is a representation of the City's achievement in silver and enamels, is set a gold medallion the border of which bears the inscriptions FOUNDED MCCCCXVIII and INCORPORATED MDLXXI and within which is a raised representation of the Company's arms (shield, helm, crest and mantling). Beneath in gold lettering on a blue enamel scroll is shown the Company's motto.

DATE OF MANUFACTURE AND DETAILS OF ANY HALLMARKS

NAME OF SILVERSMITH AND DESIGNER

SPECIAL REMARKS
Known as the Master's Medal of Office

MASTER'S CHAIN
There is a chain for the Master's Badge

OTHER BADGES
Upper Warden
Renter Warden
Past Masters
Immediate Past Master
Court Assistants
Stewards
Clerk

The Worshipful Company of
WEAVERS

DESCRIPTION OF UPPER BAILIFF'S BADGE

Set within an open gold rectangular frame each side of which is composed of a bowed arch, is set a representation of the Company's shield of arms in enamel and gold displayed on an oval shield that is encased in an ornate border of gold. Above which is a gold representation of the Company's crest upon a wreath in enamel from which decorative mantling in enamel frames the shield. Beneath, on a scroll of white enamel, is the motto in red 'Weave Truth with Trust'. All is pendant from a gold ring inset with the shield of the City's arms.

DATE OF MANUFACTURE AND DETAILS OF ANY HALLMARKS

1878

NAME OF SILVERSMITH AND DESIGNER

Metcalf and Company

SPECIAL REMARKS

Engraved on reverse 'Presented to the Worshipful Company by Frederic Ouvry (Upper Bailiff 1878)'

UPPER BAILIFF'S CHAIN

Upper Bailiff's chain presented to the Company by Col. C.R. Wigan (Upper Bailiff 1947-8, 1955-6)

OTHER BADGES

Renter Bailiff's Badge (1881) presented by Nathaniel Humphreys

Renter Warden's Badge and Upper Warden's Badge (1930) presented by the Livery to mark the Company's octocentenary

Clerk's Badge (1981) designed and made by Christopher Lawrence

LANA SPES NOSTRA

THE WORSHIPFUL · COMPANY · OF · WOOLMEN ·

The Worshipful Company of
WOOLMEN

DESCRIPTION OF MASTER'S BADGE

In a silver gilt oval suspended from a clasp depicting two crossed shepherd's crooks beneath a ram's head, within an outer border of patterned silver gilt is another border of blue enamel bearing the words THE WORSHIPFUL COMPANY OF WOOLMEN, the letters composed of brilliant diamonds, surrounding a representation of the Company's coat of arms modelled in high relief in gilt and enamels.

DATE OF MANUFACTURE AND DETAILS OF ANY HALLMARKS

1964 (replacing earlier badge of 1880)

NAME OF SILVERSMITH AND DESIGNER

SPECIAL REMARKS

The Master's Badge was stolen and (according to some sources) apparently replaced in 1970/1. Elsewhere (on the reverse of the badge) is engraved 'Presented by Past Master B.C. King 30th October 1964'.
The 1880 original was presented by Past Master William Rudge.

MASTER'S CHAIN

Pre-1973 comprising two gold (?) chains linking 11 wool packs at regular intervals

OTHER BADGES

Immediate Past Master
Past Masters
Clerk
Court Assistants (presented April 2011)

The Worshipful Company of
SCRIVENERS

DESCRIPTION OF MASTER'S BADGE

On a heavy 18ct gold ornate openwork frame topped with gold rods and eleven diamonds arranged in a fan shape is set the full achievement of the Company's arms, the supporters modelled in heavy relief in gold and coloured enamels standing on a white enamelled scroll bearing the motto. Unusually, this is repeated on a similar, smaller scroll above the crest. The shield of blue enamel is set with the charges modelled in gold and coloured enamels above which is the crest set on a torse all in coloured enamels.

DATE OF MANUFACTURE AND DETAILS OF ANY HALLMARKS

1879

NAME OF SILVERSMITH AND DESIGNER

G. Lambert

SPECIAL REMARKS

In 1930 the Court resolved that the Master's Badge be repaired and the chain lengthened at a cost of £60.10.0 and that the names of Past Masters be engraved on the shields of the chain.

MASTER'S CHAIN

OTHER BADGES

The Upper Warden's, the Renter Warden's and the Clerk's Badges (presented by Edwin Courtenay Walker, Master 1928-9)

The Notorial Deputy's (a post peculiar to the Scriveners) Badge presented in 2006 by William Brignall Kennair, Master 2008-9

The Worshipful Company of
FRUITERERS

DESCRIPTION OF MASTER'S BADGE

The shield of the Company's arms is depicted in enamel and raised 18ct gold above the Company's motto and the date 1660 (the date of the Charter) in gold on a white enamel ribbon beneath which is a rounded rectangular enamel plaque depicting St Paul preaching in Athens. All containing within a pierced border of vine leaves and grapes worked in gold and jewels, all surmounted by a large emerald and four rubies. It hangs from a loop formed of the arms of the City.

DATE OF MANUFACTURE AND DETAILS OF ANY HALLMARKS

1955 (replacing earlier badge of 1899, which itself replaced original of 1865)

NAME OF SILVERSMITH AND DESIGNER

1865 badge: Mr Biden of Cheapside
1955 badge: A Kimmance through George Gowland, London.

SPECIAL REMARKS

The Company history records that 'in June 1865 the Court resolved that a subscription be set on foot among the Members of the Court for providing a distinguishing badge for the Master at an expense of not exceeding Twenty Guineas and that in the event of the sum subscribed not being sufficient, the deficiency not exceeding Ten Pounds to be made up out of the funds of the Company.' The design that was approved had to conform to the Company's seal.

In June 1899 the Court accepted 'with cordial thanks the handsome and artistic badge presented to the Company by W.S. Steel (Past Master)'. This badge was reported lost when the Master's home was burgled in May 1955. Although there existed a plaster cast of the lost badge it was decided to accept a new design rather than make a replica of the old. The new badge was covered by the insurance value of the stolen badge (£425).

MASTER'S CHAIN

There is no chain; the badge is suspended from a ribbon embroidered with fruit (by the Royal School of Needlework)

OTHER BADGES

Upper Warden, Renter Warden
Past Masters, Honorary Assistants
The Clerk
All (save the Assistants who wear the badge on the breast pocket) are worn around the neck

The Worshipful Company of
PLAISTERERS

DESCRIPTION OF MASTER'S BADGE
On a scalloped-edged gold plate, the base formed into a scroll bearing the motto, is set the full achievement of the Company's arms with the supporters, helm, crest and mantling modelled in deep relief in gold and enamel work and with the flat shield depicting the arms in full colour enamel.

DATE OF MANUFACTURE AND DETAILS OF ANY HALLMARKS
1872

NAME OF SILVERSMITH AND DESIGNER

SPECIAL REMARKS
Purchased by the Company in July 1872

MASTER'S CHAIN
Presented by Col. Frank Griffith (Master 1910-11) to commemorate the Coronation of H.M. King George V

OTHER BADGES
2 Wardens
Clerk
Past Masters
Court Assistants
Stewards
Chaplain
Beadle

The Worshipful Company of
STATIONERS AND NEWSPAPER MAKERS

DESCRIPTION OF MASTER'S BADGE

On an open gold frame of foliage and filigree work is set the achievement of the Company's arms (without helm) depicted in gold, silver and enamel work, the supporters standing on a red enamel scroll bearing the Company motto in gilt lettering

DATE OF MANUFACTURE AND DETAILS OF ANY HALLMARKS

1878

NAME OF SILVERSMITH AND DESIGNER

Messrs Lambert

SPECIAL REMARKS

Commissioned by the Court in July 1878 following the recommendation of 'The Master's Badge Committee' at a cost of 70 guineas. In the Wardens' accounts is recorded 'paid 18th November 1878 [to] Messrs Lambert for Master's Badge £73.10. –d'.

MASTER'S CHAIN

There is a chain comprised of four strands of gold upon which are laid alternate representations of red enamel heraldic roses centred on gold open foliage and displayed eagles from the arms. The lowest link represents an open book from which is suspended the badge.

OTHER BADGES

Master's Travelling Badge (a cheaper facsimile)
Wardens
Clerk
Past Masters
Master's Wife

OMNIA DESUPER

The Worshipful Company of
BRODERERS

DESCRIPTION OF MASTER'S BADGE

The Company's shield of arms in blue and white enamels and the charges in heavy relief in gold depicted on a golden oval and surmounted by the Company's crest with the Company's motto beneath in blue lettering on a gold scroll and to either side the Company's supporters in gold and enamel.

DATE OF MANUFACTURE AND DETAILS OF ANY HALLMARKS

1874 (supporters added in 1980)

NAME OF SILVERSMITH AND DESIGNER

Not known

SPECIAL REMARKS

The reverse is engraved 'Presented to the Worshipful Company of Broderers by Charles Leaf Esqr one of the Court of Assistants Decr 1874 Gilbert C. Northcote Master'. Mr Leaf had been Master some years earlier. The supporters were added in 1980 being the gift of Past Master Anthony J. Hart, OBE, DSC, although supporters formed part of the original grant of arms in 1558. The badge is known as the Master's Jewel.

MASTER'S CHAIN

There is no chain to the Master's Badge which hangs by a ribbon that has been embroidered by the Royal School of Needlework and was a gift of Past Master M. Alan Hissey (Master 2004-5).

OTHER BADGES

The Warden's and Renter Warden's Badges presented by Sq. Leader Levy (Master 1962-3)
The Senior Past Master's Badge
Master's Lady's Brooch
The Chaplain's Badge
The Clerk's Badge
Court Assistants' Badge
Past Masters' Badge

The Worshipful Company of
UPHOLDERS

DESCRIPTION OF MASTER'S BADGE

Set on a silver cushion modelled in three dimensions and displayed diagonally and surrounded with gold braid is depicted in precious metals and enamels the full achievement of arms of the Company.

DATE OF MANUFACTURE AND DETAILS OF ANY HALLMARKS

c. 2000 (replacing badge of 1963 which itself replaced the original of 1876)

NAME OF SILVERSMITH AND DESIGNER

Not known

SPECIAL REMARKS

The badge bears on its reverse the inscription 'The MASTER'S BADGE To Commemorate The Millennium. Presented by C F Hayman, Master 1989-90, A V Kinsey, Master 1991-2 B E Chapman, Master Elect 20 January 2000'.

Whilst the Company was granted arms in 1465 it was not until 1963 that supporters and a motto were added. A new badge for the Master comprising the full achievement was presented by P. Tyson Woodstock TD, Master 1963, replacing that of 1876 which is now the Senior Warden's Badge. The 1963 badge was lost and a new badge was commissioned in 2000 and it was agreed this should commemorate the Millennium. Subsequently, the 1963 badge was recovered and was employed as a Badge of Office by the Warden to the Trade.

MASTER'S CHAIN

A chain of two strands in silver-gilt with 24 spacers. The oval clasp is inscribed 'Presented by A.W. Schuster MBE, Master 1958'.

OTHER BADGES

The Senior and Junior Wardens have badges, the former almost certainly the original Master's Badge dating from 1876 as it bears the enamelled coat of arms of the donor, Edward Hunter, Master 1876.

The Warden to the Trade wears the Master's Badge of 1963.

Court Assistants, The Clerk, Chaplain, Steward, Past Masters, Badges for Master's, Senior Warden's and Junior Warden's Ladies.

The Worshipful Company of
MUSICIANS

DESCRIPTION OF MASTER'S BADGE

A shield bearing the arms of the Company in enamel and gold with the charges in raised gold and enamel
work and beneath a scroll bearing the motto in blue enamel on gold.

The Company's motto is 'Preserve Harmony', here reduced to the single word, 'Harmony'.

The torse (striped gold and blue) at the head of the shield would normally have the crest above, which, for
the Musicians' Company, is a lyre. Perhaps this element of the badge has been lost in years past?

DATE OF MANUFACTURE AND DETAILS OF ANY HALLMARKS

1879

NAME OF SILVERSMITH AND DESIGNER

SPECIAL REMARKS

On 8 July 1879 the Court approved the sum of £28 to be spent on the purchase of the Master's Badge.

The swan in the arms is indicative of a link with Apollo, the patron god of music and poetry in classical
mythology. However, it was also the personal badge of George Carey, 2nd Baron Hunsdon. He was Lord
Chamberlain and an amateur musician who died in 1603 and it may be that the arms granted to the
Company in 1604 included this tribute to the memory of a renowned patron of the arts.

MASTER'S CHAIN

Chain of Office presented on 27 October 1908 by Mr Crews

OTHER BADGES

Senior and Junior Wardens Badges (1879)

Clerk, Immediate Past Master, Court Assistants and Past Masters. There is also a Lady's Brooch, which the
Master's lady uses during his year

The Worshipful Company of
TURNERS

DESCRIPTION OF MASTER'S BADGE

Worked in silver gilt and enamel, in the form of a quatrefoil medallion framing a central imposing and finely enamelled three dimensional figure of Saint Catherine between two enamelled shields bearing the arms of the City of London and the Company respectively, the charges thereon in heavy relief in gold, silver and enamel. Beneath which is a scroll of white enamel inscribed with the Company's motto in gold.

DATE OF MANUFACTURE AND DETAILS OF ANY HALLMARKS

21 July 1877

NAME OF SILVERSMITH AND DESIGNER

Designed by Mr Shoppe, who was responsible for the design of a number of Masters' Badges

SPECIAL REMARKS

At a Court held on 21 July 1877 'Deputy Controller Bake stated that at a meeting of some of the livery … [it was resolved] …

'That for the purpose of testifying in a lasting form their appreciation of the great services rendered by the Court of Assistants in the cause of Technical Education, a Master's Badge of Office be executed … and presented to the Court'.

MASTER'S CHAIN

A collar-chain of 15ct gold wire and leaf pattern flexible links with the monogram T.C. in the centre. Presented to the Company in 1905 by Past Master Cecil Maitland Bevan, as a memento of his year of office.

OTHER BADGES

Upper Warden's Badge of silver gilt and enamel presented by C.H.J. Day (Master 1935) and a Renter
  Warden's Badge
The Clerk's Badge was made in 1964

The Worshipful Company of
BASKETMAKERS

DESCRIPTION OF PRIME WARDEN'S BADGE

Yellow metal and enamel, shaped oval scroll pattern bearing the Company's motto at its head, suspended from a cast and enamelled Company crest, with a central oval gold-coloured and enamel plaque of the Company's arms, partially covering an inclined red and white enamelled City arms to the left and County of Middlesex arms in red and gold enamel to the right, pierced through with crossed mace and sword and the City motto beneath.

DATE OF MANUFACTURE AND DETAILS OF ANY HALLMARKS

1916 – re-modelled and repaired in 1961. Weight 349 g. The 1916 badge replaced an earlier version of 1886 which was deposited with the Guildhall Museum (now in the Museum of London).

NAME OF SILVERSMITH AND DESIGNER

Not known

SPECIAL REMARKS

The first badge was commissioned by the Court from Company funds (not to exceed £15) in October 1886.
The current badge is engraved on the reverse 'Presented by Mr & Mrs J.N.C. White To The Worshipful
    Company of Basket Makers May it flourish root and branch.'
Presumably the official description uses the term 'yellow metal' because there are no hallmarks but it would
    be reasonable to infer that the badge is of gold or silver gilt.

PRIME WARDEN'S CHAIN

A very fine Prime Warden's collarette was also presented by Mrs White in 1916. The gold chain, a family heirloom, which had served as a Sheriff's chain about 60 years earlier, consists of finely shaped links, each elaborately engraved.

OTHER BADGES

Prime Warden's Undress Badge was presented in 1933 by Major Richard Rigg (perhaps following the formal grant of arms in 1931) and is suspended from an embroidered collaret. There are badges for Upper and Under Wardens (1997), Chaplain (1900), Hon. Trade Adviser and Clerk, the last presented in 1949.

LUCEM TUAM DA NOBIS O DEUS

The Worshipful Company of
GLAZIERS AND PAINTERS OF GLASS

DESCRIPTION OF MASTER'S BADGE

An 18ct gold and enamel badge of oval form, the cast and chased decoration depicting the Company's crest and supporters within a studded strap and buckle, inset with an oval enamel depicting the shield of arms above an applied enamel scroll inscribed with the Company's motto.

DATE OF MANUFACTURE AND DETAILS OF ANY HALLMARKS

1900 (replacing original of 1875)
Maker's mark: IMS London 1900

NAME OF SILVERSMITH AND DESIGNER

Spink and Son

SPECIAL REMARKS

On 21 September 1875 the Master produced to the Court a jewel appropriate for the Master, the price of which he stated to be £14.14.0 and it was resolved that it should be purchased. It was in 9ct gold and enamels and is now worn by the Deputy Master.

In 1900 the Master, Benjamin Scott McGough, presented to the Company a Master's Jewel to be held in perpetuity. It is engraved on the reverse 'Master's Badge. Presented to the Worshipful Company of Glaziers by B S Foster-McGough, Esq CC JP on his accession to office 30th Novr 1900'. The arms show a lion passant guardant in chief, for that was the version used until a certificate was issued by Garter King of Arms in 1926 which confirmed that the proper version was a demi-lion passant guardant.

MASTER'S CHAIN

There is no chain

OTHER BADGES

Deputy Master (original Master's Badge of 1875)
Upper Warden, Renter Warden (1933 Maker's Mark DCC Birmingham)
Past Masters
Senior Assistants (former Upper Warden's Badge)
Assistants
Hon. Treasurer, Hon. Curator, Hon. Solicitor, Stewards, Clerk, Hon. Chaplain (Former Renter Warden's Badge)

The Worshipful Company of
HORNERS

DESCRIPTION OF MASTER'S BADGE

Upon a representation of the Polyethylene Molecule depicted in black enamel on silver on a further scalloped polygon plaque is placed a three dimensional silver demi-ram guardant supporting between its forelegs a representation of the Benzene ring in black between which is shown a Narwhal tusk and over the lower part of the ram is a shield à couché bearing the Company's arms.

DATE OF MANUFACTURE AND DETAILS OF ANY HALLMARKS

1992 (replacing earlier badge of 1880)
No hallmarks apparent

NAME OF SILVERSMITH AND DESIGNER

Sir David Hughes, Bt. of Wilburton, Cambs. (having purchased the firm of A E Lejeune in 1979)

SPECIAL REMARKS

On the reverse is engraved '7 October 1993 Presented by Donald du Parc Braham Master 1991 – 1992 The year of the Grant of New Armorial Bearings to the Company'.

The earlier badge is now worn by the Deputy Master and is engraved on the reverse 'Presented by a Warden of the Company February 2nd 1880'.

MASTER'S CHAIN

There is a chain

OTHER BADGES

Mistress's Brooch, being a smaller exact replica of the Master's Badge engraved on the reverse: Presented by
Jeremy D. Spofforth Master 1993-4
Deputy Master (see above)

The Worshipful Company of
FARRIERS

DESCRIPTION OF MASTER'S BADGE

The Company's shield in white enamel with the horseshoes in gold inlaid with diamonds rests on a gold oval band supported by the Company's supporters in gold, standing on a compartment of gold and blue enamel and a scroll of gold with the motto depicted in diamonds and all surmounted by the helm in gold supporting the crest in coloured enamels.

DATE OF MANUFACTURE AND DETAILS OF ANY HALLMARKS

1874

NAME OF SILVERSMITH AND DESIGNER

It is conjectured that Horatio Stewart (see below) might be the same man who was a partner in Hancocks & Co. (Gold and Silversmiths) at about the time of manufacture. If so, he would certainly have been in a perfect position to have the badge made and subsequently embellished with additional jewels.

SPECIAL REMARKS

On 9 November 1874 the Court minutes record: 'It had been necessary that a proper badge should be executed for the Master and Wardens and Mr Horatio Stewart requested he be allowed to present a suitable badge for the Master which was gratefully accepted.' He had jewels added to the original badge in 1878.

MASTER'S CHAIN

Presented by J.R. Cooper in 1882

OTHER BADGES

Wardens and Past Masters
Clerk's Badge (2009 replacing one from 1915)
In 1883 the Court produced a badge in the form of round silver medals bearing the Company's arms (at £4)
    to be adopted for wear by Members of the Court not past the Chair
Simple badges for Liverymen and Freemen

The Worshipful Company of
PAVIORS

DESCRIPTION OF MASTER'S BADGE

The upper part of the badge shows the full achievement of the Company's arms in coloured enamels against a gold backboard. The supporters stand on a paved ground complete with a basket of stones and a pig walking on the newly paved surface. To the side are featured picks and shovels and three significant dates in the Company's history: 1302, 1479 and 1929. The arms are set upon two gold medallions showing street works in progress in the Middle Ages and a coach and horses travelling along a well paved street.

DATE OF MANUFACTURE AND DETAILS OF ANY HALLMARKS

Post 1942 (replacing 1933 badge which itself replaced original of 1889)

NAME OF SILVERSMITH AND DESIGNER

SPECIAL REMARKS

The original badge was presented in 1889 by Mr ex-Sheriff George Burt. This was replaced in 1933 (the gift of Major E.J. Burt) to depict more properly the Company's arms after they were regularised by the College of Arms in November 1929. It was designed by Bernard Gribble and made by the Goldsmiths & Silversmiths Company. The old Master's Badge was remodelled for use by the Upper Warden. The new Master's Badge was lost in enemy action in 1942 and the present badge replaces this.

MASTER'S CHAIN

Chain presented in 1890 by J.J. Griffiths

OTHER BADGES

Wardens, Past Master, Clerk, Mistress Pavior (Master's Lady), Court Assistants, Court Emeritus, Liverymen, Freemen, Hon Freemen

The Worshipful Company of
LORINERS

Description of Master's Badge

Within a spur shaped 9ct gold frame is offset to the dexter the shield of the Company's arms in blue and white enamel with the charges modelled in gold. Behind the shield is a rearing horse in gold. Above is an open shield shape containing the arms of the City in gold and white and red enamel.

Date of Manufacture and Details of any Hallmarks

1990 (replacing an earlier Badge that was stolen)

Name of Silversmith and Designer

Designed by David Thomas (Liveryman of the Goldsmiths' Company)

Special Remarks

The Badge was commissioned in 1990 to replace the original that had been stolen. It was first worn by Robert Walker-Arnott, for a few minutes at the Installation Court in January 1991 before he handed it to his successor as Master, Bill Willson-Pemberton.
The designer was sent a sample spur to use as a model for his design.

Master's Chain

The chain was presented by brothers Douglas, Hugh and Alan Walker-Arnott at the end of their three-year run as Masters (presumably) at the January Court of 1968.

Other Badges

2 Wardens' Badges
Immediate Past Master
The Clerk

The Worshipful Society of
APOTHECARIES

DESCRIPTION OF MASTER'S BADGE

The Society's arms are depicted in enamel and gold and silver and set upon an elaborate pierced fleur-de-lis and scrollwork in gold studded with diamonds. The supporters are modelled in high relief in gold and the shield is of blue enamel with the charge thereon also depicted in high relief.

DATE OF MANUFACTURE AND DETAILS OF ANY HALLMARKS

1987 (replacing stolen original dating from 1919-20)

NAME OF SILVERSMITH AND DESIGNER

Garrards

SPECIAL REMARKS

The Master's Jewel was stolen from the Hall on 24 February 1987 and an identical replacement, funded by the insurance claim, was made by Garrards. The original was presented by Samuel Osborn, Master 1919-20. In earlier times the Master and Wardens wore gilded crowns on feast days.

MASTER'S CHAIN

The Master's chain was presented in 2003 by former Lord Mayor (Apothecary and Barber) Sir John Chalstrey and was his shrieval chain in 1993-4.

OTHER BADGES

There are also jewels for: The Immediate Past Master, Senior Warden, Junior Warden, the President of the Faculty of History and Philosophy of Medicine & Pharmacy (1960 Garrards) and the Master's Lady; and lesser badges for Clerk, the Registrar, Assistant Clerk, Chaplain and Chairman of the Livery Committee.

The Worshipful Company of
SHIPWRIGHTS

DESCRIPTION OF PRIME WARDEN'S BADGE

The Company's full achievement of arms in gold and enamel, the charges on the shield in gold in high relief. The two supporters standing on a scroll bearing the Company's motto in gold letters on blue enamel and beneath which is shown the full arms of the City in gold all upon sprigs of laurel in gold.

DATE OF MANUFACTURE AND DETAILS OF ANY HALLMARKS

1876 (remade 1882 and supporters added subsequently)

NAME OF SILVERSMITH AND DESIGNER

Designed and worked by Maurice Emanuel (a Portsmouth silversmith)

SPECIAL REMARKS

At a Court held on 24 February 1876 'it was resolved unanimously that a Master's Badge be procured at an expense not to exceed £52.10.0d.' The final invoice from Maurice Emanuel exceeded this sum by £10 10s. but it is not recorded how the matter was settled. In 1878 it was reported that the badge had been altered, at his own expense, by James R. Brown, a manufacturing goldsmith and member of the Company, 'so that the shield of arms accord with the Grant …' The reverse is engraved 'MASTER'S BADGE ¦ The Worshipful Company ¦ of ¦ Shipwrights ¦ George Tatum Eqsuire, MASTER ¦ William Broomham Esquire ¦ WARDENS ¦ William S Page Esquire ¦ 22nd MARCH 1876'.

Variations to the Company's arms necessitated further alterations to the badge in 1882, 1920 and 1982 when David Thomas, a Chelsea goldsmith, made the necessary adjustments. This is recorded with the inscription 'Remade incorporating supporters 1984'.

In 1932 HRH The Duke of York became the first Permanent Master and the Master became known as the Second Master, and later as the Prime Warden.

PRIME WARDEN'S CHAIN

2 rows of 24ct gold links joined by reef knots with at the foot a clasp in the form of a dolphin from which the badge may be suspended. Presented by Maj. Gen. G.S. Szlumper, CBE 1947-8. The inner row presented by Sir W. Nicholas Cayzer 1967.

OTHER BADGES

Permanent Master 18ct gold with enamel: Made by P.G. Dodd & Son 1932 Designed by Bernard Gribble

Past Prime Warden's Badge	Past Prime Warden's Lady's Jewel
Wardens' Badges	Hon Treasurer's Badge
Prime Warden's Lady's Jewel	Clerk's Badge

The Worshipful Company of
SPECTACLE MAKERS

DESCRIPTION OF MASTER'S BADGE

The full achievement of the Company's arms is depicted in a modern style in gold and enamel work set upon an open decorated frame of gold with a scroll at the base beneath the compartment in blue and white enamel bearing the legend WORSHIPFUL COMPANY OF SPECTACLE MAKERS

Overall dimensions 105mm x 90mm

Gross weight 13.5 grams

DATE OF MANUFACTURE AND DETAILS OF ANY HALLMARKS

London 1991 (replacing earlier badges)

NAME OF SILVERSMITH AND DESIGNER

J.H. O'Dell

SPECIAL REMARKS

The arms were granted in 1950 and a new badge commissioned which is currently used by the Deputy Master when the current badge was wrought in 1991. Prior to the grant of arms the Company used a 'pseudoheraldic device' and the original Master's Badge (presented 1 July 1869) bore this design. It was lost during an air raid in the Second World War.

MASTER'S CHAIN

A modern hallmarked silver gilt Chain of Office incorporating 58 stylised shield shaped links each replicating the shield from the Company's achievement of arms: dated 1982 and weighing 380 grams.

OTHER BADGES

Deputy Master (previously Master's Badge)

Upper Warden – this badge bears the original 'pseudoheraldic device'

Renter Warden

Clerk

Court Assistants

Liverymen

The Worshipful Company of
CLOCKMAKERS

DESCRIPTION OF MASTER'S BADGE

The arms of the Company are shown in gold, silver and enamel work, the supporters standing on a scroll bearing the motto, all on an ornamental and heavily worked gold roundel.

DATE OF MANUFACTURE AND DETAILS OF ANY HALLMARKS

1924 (replacing original of 1873)

NAME OF SILVERSMITH AND DESIGNER

SPECIAL REMARKS

In 1873 the Court commented on the desirability of providing a badge for the Master and Mr Parker, a Member of the Court, laid before the Court a design for the same. It was agreed to have one made in 18ct gold and enamel at an expense not exceeding £60. The original badge was lost on a bus on London Bridge in 1924. The then Master fined himself heavily and the insurers also paid £125. A committee comprising Henry Gayden, Percy Webster and Sir David Salomons was set up to recommend designs and the current badge was commissioned. The original turned up in the 1960s and was presented back to the Company. It is now in the possession of the Clockmakers' Museum at Guildhall. Other copies are at the Museum of London.

MASTER'S CHAIN

Sir David Salomons presented a heavy three-strand gold chain to enhance the new badge (1924). It had been the shrieval chain of his uncle in 1835. In 1963 this chain was presented to Gilbert Edgar to use as his own shrieval chain. In return he donated a new chain for the Master which incorporated some of the links from the Salomon chain.

OTHER BADGES

Wardens' Badges (1874)
Clerk
Past Masters
Court Assistants (who wear the livery medal with a clasp)

The Worshipful Company of
GLOVERS

DESCRIPTION OF MASTER'S BADGE

A silver gilt laurel wreath surrounding a silver gilt and enamel circlet bearing the legend 'THE WORSHIPFUL COMPANY OF GLOVERS OF LONDON' encircling a representation in silver gilt and enamels of the Company's achievement of arms.

DATE OF MANUFACTURE AND DETAILS OF ANY HALLMARKS

1990
Replacement for the original destroyed by enemy action in 1941
Hallmarked

NAME OF SILVERSMITH AND DESIGNER

SPECIAL REMARKS

The original badge probably dated from *c.*1886 when the Company was revitalised. The present badge is engraved on reverse 'Presented by Past Master Clive Lidstone MBE to the Worshipful Company of Glovers of London April 1990'.

MASTER'S CHAIN

There is a chain

OTHER BADGES

Wardens
Clerk
Past Masters

DECUS ET TUTAMEN

The Worshipful Company of FELTMAKERS

DESCRIPTION OF MASTER'S BADGE

Within a decorated gold octofoil border embellished with six semi-precious stones are set accollée the shields of the City (to the dexter) and the Company in pierced gold and coloured enamels (to the sinister) below which is the Company's motto in coloured enamel and above both the helm, mantling and crest of the Company in silver and enamels.

DATE OF MANUFACTURE AND DETAILS OF ANY HALLMARKS

1892

NAME OF SILVERSMITH AND DESIGNER

SPECIAL REMARKS

In 1892 funds were raised by the Court for a Master's Badge at a cost of £37.10.0. At the same time a duplicate was made that was lodged with the Guildhall Museum, though it has since been returned to the Company.

MASTER'S CHAIN

There is no chain

OTHER BADGES

Past Masters' Badges were introduced in 1894
There are badges for the Wardens and the Clerk

The Worshipful Company of
FRAMEWORK KNITTERS

DESCRIPTION OF MASTER'S BADGE
Within a decorated quatrefoil elongated oval on a blue enamel background are depicted the shield, crest, motto and supporters of the Company's arms in raised gold and enamel work.

DATE OF MANUFACTURE AND DETAILS OF ANY HALLMARKS
1881
(No hallmarks visible)

NAME OF SILVERSMITH AND DESIGNER

SPECIAL REMARKS
The Master's Jewel was commissioned by the Court at a cost of £48 and is inscribed on the reverse: 'Master Arthur Risdon Capel, Esq ¦ Wardens Richard William Bohm Esq ¦ Richard Worthington Esq ¦ 23rd March AD 1881'.

MASTER'S CHAIN
A silver gilt and enamel ceremonial chain. Hallmarked London 1894
Maker: H.T. Lamb

OTHER BADGES
Master's Travelling Badge presented by R.B. Osborne (Master 1997-8)
Wardens' Badges – Silver gilt and enamel of vessica shape in the form of a medieval seal. Hallmarked London 1897 Maker: H.T. Lamb
Clerk's and Assistant Clerk's Badges
The Master's Lady has a jewel presented by Past Master Martin

The Worshipful Company of
NEEDLEMAKERS

DESCRIPTION OF MASTER'S BADGE

Silver gilt and enamel: within an open gold circle are shown the arms of the Company raised in gold and enamel. The motto is shown below in green enamel on white. The circle itself is set within an open oval entwined with scrolls and leaves with a pointed lobe at the top to fasten to the ribbon or chain. The arms of the Company are unusual in that they are displayed in front of an apple tree entwined by a serpent (as shown in the badge).

DATE OF MANUFACTURE AND DETAILS OF ANY HALLMARKS

1986 (replacing original of 1874 and perhaps an earlier badge of 1800)
Hallmarked

NAME OF SILVERSMITH AND DESIGNER

Toye, Kenning and Spencer, Birmingham

SPECIAL REMARKS

The Court commissioned silver gilt medals for the Court in 1777. Clearly the Master wore one but it is not recorded if this were as Master or as a Court Member though circumstantial evidence seems to show that in 1800 the new Master's name replaced an earlier name on the medal. The 1874 badge was commissioned after the 'revival' of the Company by 'gentlemen of substance'.

The new jewel was made because of the alteration in the arms of the Company on the occasion of the grant of arms by the College of Arms in September 1986.

The cost of £2,200 was raised by subscription from the Court of Assistants.

MASTER'S CHAIN

The chain was commissioned to replace one dating from 1932 that was stolen in 1988. The purchase price of £5,750 was part covered by insurance and part the gift of Past Master P.L. Barrows. It was created by Jacqueline Grüber Steiger of Welton, East Yorkshire. Hallmarked Sheffield 1990.

OTHER BADGES

Jewel of Master's Wife
Immediate Past Master
Past Masters
Hon. Archivist
Clerk

The Worshipful Company of
GARDENERS

DESCRIPTION OF MASTER'S BADGE

The shield of the Company's arms in coloured enamels is set below the Company's crest in gold and enamel and between its supporters in gold, all on a decorative blue enamel circle set within a border of red enamel with the Company's motto in gold. All this is within an elaborate decorated gold border, topped by the City's shield in enamel.

DATE OF MANUFACTURE AND DETAILS OF ANY HALLMARKS

1892

NAME OF SILVERSMITH AND DESIGNER

Designed by George Edwards

SPECIAL REMARKS

At a Court held on 20 May 1891 it was decided to provide a Badge of Office for the Master and on 16 December 1891 a design by George Edwards was approved at a cost of £75. The reverse is engraved 'Worshipful Company of Gardeners London (Incorporated 1615) The Master's Badge 1892'.

In 1903 Mr Ebblewhite reported to the Court that the badges of Master, Wardens and Clerk differed from those tricked (sketched) in the Charter of James I and it was agreed to have this put right.

MASTER'S CHAIN

The Master's chain was presented in April 1902 by the Master, Mr C.E. Osman. It comprises 58 shields with elaborate links and each showing either a monogram or a crest or an achievement of a Past Master. The 59th and lowest link depicts the Company's shield.

OTHER BADGES

Upper Warden, Renter Warden, Clerk

These three badges in silver gilt were presented by W.T. Crosweller in 1897 as a memento of the Queen's Diamond Jubilee

Past Masters

Spadebearer

Court Assistants

The *Worshipful Company of*
TIN PLATE WORKERS

DESCRIPTION OF MASTER'S BADGE
A modern three-coloured 18ct gold and enamel badge of lozenge shape with an enamelled depiction of the Company's arms all within a wirework border

DATE OF MANUFACTURE AND DETAILS OF ANY HALLMARKS
London 1970 (replacing an earlier version)

NAME OF SILVERSMITH AND DESIGNER
George Attenborough & Son

SPECIAL REMARKS
The gift of Harold Charles Hobbs, a Past Master of the Company, to commemorate the 300th Anniversary of the incorporation of the Company and presented on that occasion.

It is of note that the Company received a grant of arms in 1957 regularising arms used unofficially before that date.

MASTER'S CHAIN
Also the gift of H.C. Hobbs, an 18ct gold collar with alternating oblong and wire scroll motifs heightened with oblong enamelling with the arms of the Past Masters suspending a medallion enamelled with the arms of the Company and suspending a shield enamelled with the arms of the City of London. 1970.

OTHER BADGES
Master's Lady
2 Wardens
Deputy Master
Past Masters
Court Assistants
The Clerk
Hon. Chaplain
3 Stewards
Liverymen

The Worshipful Company of
WHEELWRIGHTS

DESCRIPTION OF MASTER'S BADGE

On a circle of blue enamel with a rim of 18ct gold is set a shaped golden plaque upon which is rendered in high relief the Company's full achievement of arms in gold and silver and white, yellow and green enamel. Around the outside of the gold circle are set 16 wheels in gold and alternating white and red enamel, each wheel set within a golden decorative U (crescent) with tapering ends. Beneath the shield is a scroll of gold and blue enamel bearing the Company's motto in gold letters and at the head of the badge is a representation of the shield, supporters and motto of the City in gold and enamel.

DATE OF MANUFACTURE AND DETAILS OF ANY HALLMARKS

1873
76 grams gross weight

NAME OF SILVERSMITH AND DESIGNER

SPECIAL REMARKS

In 1873 the Court resolved to provide a badge for the Master at a cost of not more than 50 guineas. The first design was not approved but later in the year a second badge was accepted and first worn at a Livery Dinner in October 1873. The reverse engraved 'The badge for the use of the Master of the Worshipful Company of Wheelwrights was first worn at The Master's and Livery Dinner 14th October 1873. Jas. Saunders Esq, W.Foster, Esq. Jas. R. Scott, Esq.'

MASTER'S CHAIN

Executed in 9ct gold and comprising 27 links, each pierced and decorated in blue enamel as a wheel within pierced flat foliate borders alternating with a stud and double flower-head spacers, the whole with two clips and attached to a red/yellow silk ribbon. This was presented by Charles Dew Miller, Master, 1885. There is also an 'outdoor' chain worn only with the gown, being silver gilt and enamel (Birmingham 1969 Toye, Kenning & Spencer) comprising 21 circular links each with a maroon enamel 8-spoke wheel at the centre.

OTHER BADGES

Two Warden's Badges in 18ct gold and enamel presented by A.E. Aldridge (Master 1887-8)
Clerk's Badge in 9ct gold and enamel presented by Michael H. Hinton & Lt. Col. G. Bates (Master 1966)
Past Masters' Badges were approved in 1886 for 7 guineas with 4/6 extra allocated for the inscriptions.

The Worshipful Company of
DISTILLERS

DESCRIPTION OF MASTER'S BADGE

The original badge takes the form of an oval medal in gold bearing on one face the legend 'Company of Distillers of London' and the Company's arms in relief. Beneath the motto, which at various times has been rendered in different forms, but here is 'Drop as Rain – Distil as Dew', is the date '1852'. The reverse shows a head and shoulders portrait in high relief of Sir Theodore Turquet de Mayerne with the inscription of his name and Founder MDCXXXIX. Around the rim of the badge is engraved: 'PRESENTED BY GEORGE SMITH, MASTER 1851-52'.

DATE OF MANUFACTURE AND DETAILS OF ANY HALLMARKS

1852

NAME OF SILVERSMITH AND DESIGNER

SPECIAL REMARKS

The original badge was lost in the early 1980s and a new badge was presented by Past Master Walter Sichel in 1984 and is, perhaps, the work of Grant MacDonald. Subsequently the original was found and the Court directed this should be used by the Immediate Past Master.

In 2010 it was agreed to revert to the original badge for use by the Master.

The date on the original badge indicates that this is one of the earliest Master's Badges known.

MASTER'S CHAIN

An ornate chain with alternating sunbursts in gold; intertwined blue and gold scrolls bearing the Company's motto and a double-armed still – all charges from the Company's arms.

OTHER BADGES

Renter Warden
Middle Warden
Upper Warden
Mistress
Clerk
Immediate Past Master

The Worshipful Company of
PATTENMAKERS

DESCRIPTION OF MASTER'S BADGE

Enclosed within an oval buckled garter of gold and blue enamel bearing the Company's motto in gold is the shield of the Company's arms in red and white enamel and the charges in relief thereon in gold and silver. The shield is surrounded by laurel leaves in gold and enamel and surmounted by the Company's crest on its wreath in gold and enamel work. The badge is suspended from a shield of the City's arms and crest in gold and enamel.

DATE OF MANUFACTURE AND DETAILS OF ANY HALLMARKS

NAME OF SILVERSMITH AND DESIGNER

SPECIAL REMARKS

The current badge (date unknown) replaces a much earlier badge. In December 1772 the Court Minutes record: 'The Master for the time being to ware [*sic*] the Great Medal and every other Member to ware his medal during the Court sitting …' Probably this refers to the livery medals that were commissioned by the Court in March 1772. The Company has recently introduced a Livery Medal which is said to be a replica of the 1772 badge.

MASTER'S CHAIN

Gift of two Past Masters in 1965 (maker's mark 'JP')

OTHER BADGES

The Royal Patron
The Upper Warden
The Renter Warden
Warden to the Trade
Liverymen
Court Assistants

The Worshipful Company of
GLASS SELLERS

DESCRIPTION OF MASTER'S BADGE

On a blue enamel circle bordered with a circlet of silver balls are set the three charges from the Company's shield in silver together with a gilt and pink enamel scroll bearing the Company's motto in gilt letters. All are set within a quatrefoil of silver balls and four fleur de lis. This is set within a gold border showing in raised gilt letters the legend: THE WORSHIPFUL COMPANY OF GLASS SELLERS OF LONDON INCORPORATED 1664. The badge is surmounted by an elaborate scroll and the arms of the City in gold, silver and enamel.

DATE OF MANUFACTURE AND DETAILS OF ANY HALLMARKS

1922 (replacing original of 1874)
Hallmarked 1922 (?Birmingham)

NAME OF SILVERSMITH AND DESIGNER

Bradshaw & Co.

SPECIAL REMARKS

In December 1873 the Court resolved that a badge be designed to be worn by the Master for the time being: it was left to the Master and Clerk to carry out this wish and one was subsequently ordered at a cost up to £44 2s.

    This badge was stolen and on the reverse of its replacement is engraved 'MASTER'S BADGE This badge was presented to the Worshipful Company of Glass Sellers by Past Master H. Marks to replace the one stolen during his year of office 1921-22'.

MASTER'S CHAIN

There is a chain

OTHER BADGES

Prime Warden
Renter Warden
Clerk
Mistress

The Worshipful Company of
Coachmakers &
Coach Harness Makers

Description of Master's Badge
The full achievement of the Company's arms rendered in gold with the helm shown in silver.

Date of Manufacture and Details of any Hallmarks
1917

Name of Silversmith and Designer

Special Remarks
Badge presented by Reverend Honyel Gough Rosedale DD, FSA, FRSL (Master 1917)

Master's Chain
A chain for the Master was presented by the Rev. Honyel Gough Rosedale in 1917, but in 1957 the Rt. Hon. Lord Kenilworth CBE, TD, defrayed the costs of altering a chain presented by Lady Margaret Lawrence so that it could be used as the Master's chain, and also altered the 1917 chain so that it could be used by the Clerk.

Other Badges
3 Wardens' Badges given by Past Master Sir Edward Manville
Court Assistants
Clerk
Assistant Clerk

The Worshipful Company of
GUNMAKERS

DESCRIPTION OF MASTER'S BADGE

On a gold oval, enamelled in blue, is set the device used by the Company in gold and with the shield shown in white enamel, the charges thereon in gold. Beneath the shield is a scroll of diamonds.

The oval is set within an elaborate border of gold set with diamonds.

DATE OF MANUFACTURE AND DETAILS OF ANY HALLMARKS

1878 (with diamond border added in 1884)

NAME OF SILVERSMITH AND DESIGNER

SPECIAL REMARKS

On 15 November 1877, the Master, Captain D.A. Gibbs, informed the Court that he had had a badge made, which he duly presented to the Company. On 15 May 1884 the Executors of a Mr W. Payne informed the Court that Mr Payne had bequeathed a jewelled ornament to the Company with the intent that the diamond border should enclose the arms of the Company. Accordingly the following inscription was placed on the reverse of the badge 'The Arms of the Worshipful Company of Gunsmiths were presented by Captain David Aspland Gibbs Master in 1856, 1865 and 1877 and the Jewelled Frame was bequeathed by the late William John Payne, Esq, Coroner of the City of London, Master in 1858, 1866 and 1878.'

The device used by the Company at the time the badge was commissioned has now been superseded by a grant of arms of 1973.

MASTER'S CHAIN

There is no chain at the time of writing

OTHER BADGES

Upper Warden
Renter Warden
Clerk

The Worshipful Company of
GOLD AND SILVER WYRE DRAWERS

DESCRIPTION OF MASTER'S BADGE

The badge depicts the full achievement of the Company (shield, supporters, helm, crest and motto) in gold and enamelwork.

DATE OF MANUFACTURE AND DETAILS OF ANY HALLMARKS

1880
Perhaps embellished in 1886

NAME OF SILVERSMITH AND DESIGNER

Although conjecture, it seems likely that the badge was the work of George Kenning's company, he being Master in 1882/3.

SPECIAL REMARKS

The Company history records that: 'The Company had celebrated its sense of corporate splendour by buying a gold and enamel badge for the Master in 1880'.

The reverse bears the inscription: 'Worshipful Company of Gold and Silver Wyre Drawers London Master's Badge 1880' together with the names of the Master, Wardens and Clerk and 'Subscribed for by the Members of the Court of Assistants'.

There is a further engraved inscription on the reverse of the mantling mentioning a presentation from the Master in 1886 leading to the probability that the badge was enhanced (perhaps with the addition of crest and supporters at that later date.

MASTER'S CHAIN

A chain composed of gold and silver wire

OTHER BADGES

4 Wardens
Past Masters
Court Assistants
Stewards
Clerk

The Worshipful Company of
MAKERS OF PLAYING CARDS

DESCRIPTION OF MASTER'S BADGE

In pierced gold and red enamel the arms of the Company set above the date 1629 (the date of the Charter of Incorporation) within an ornate scrollwork frame.

DATE OF MANUFACTURE AND DETAILS OF ANY HALLMARKS

1951 (replacing earlier versions)

NAME OF SILVERSMITH AND DESIGNER

Thomas Fattorini

SPECIAL REMARKS

The first badge appeared in 1880 and it is believed this was deposited at Guildhall Museum when a new version was commissioned (date unknown). This lasted until the Second World War when it, and the Company's Records, were destroyed in the Blitz. A third version was used between 1942 and 1950 but was merely temporary and considered of poor quality. It was replaced in 1951, at which time a spare (or duplicate) was fashioned.

MASTER'S CHAIN

The ribbon (from which the badge is suspended) was adorned with enamelled playing cards' pip symbols (a spade, heart, club and diamond) in 1998/9 by the then Master (the late Anthony Wilcox).

OTHER BADGES

Wardens' Badges (1880)

Past Masters' Badges – introduced in October 1881 when the Past Masters were expected to buy their own, which caused something of a revolt. Now PM's Badges are owned by the Company and returned for re-issue

Clerk (1990 replacing earlier gift of PM W.E. Luke)

Stewards' Badges (1984)

The Worshipful Company of
FAN MAKERS

DESCRIPTION OF MASTER'S BADGE

The shield of the Company's arms in gold and enamel, with the Company's motto on a scroll beneath and above in gold and enamel the arms of the City surrounded by its motto above which is a representation of the Company's crest, all placed upon an inverted fan in gold. This feature makes the Fan Makers' badge most distinctive.

DATE OF MANUFACTURE AND DETAILS OF ANY HALLMARKS

Designed and purchased by the Court in 1878

NAME OF SILVERSMITH AND DESIGNER

SPECIAL REMARKS

Inscribed on reverse '1878 FAN MAKERS COMPANY MASTERS BADGE/HENRY HOMEWARD CRAWFORD ESQ MASTER/UNDER SHERIFF OF LONDON & MIDDLESEX/JOHN SUGDEN ESQ AND H.F. GRIFFIN ESQ WARDENS'

The creation of the Master's Badge coincides with the revitalisation of the Company and the increase in the number of its livery.

MASTER'S CHAIN

Presented by Deputy Richard Clarence Halse, Master 1895

OTHER BADGES

Wardens' Badges (1915 presented by A.P. Bartley in his year as Master)

Past Masters' Badges

Assistants' Badges (1962 presented by C.A.L. Collins in his year as Master)

Mistress Fan Maker's Badge (Presented by PM W.E. Arnold)

Clerk's Badge (replacing an earlier badge that was lost and which had been presented by PM A.W. Fowles)

The Worshipful Company of
CARMEN

DESCRIPTION OF MASTER'S BADGE

The arms of the Company in 18ct gold and red enamel with the motto in red lettering on a white enamel scroll all on a gold disc with finials at top, bottom, left and right projecting beyond a circlet of red enamel bearing the legends in gold lettering MASTER and WORSHIPFUL COMPANY OF CARMEN.

DATE OF MANUFACTURE AND DETAILS OF ANY HALLMARKS

1938 (replacing original of 1893)

NAME OF SILVERSMITH AND DESIGNER

Reverse inscribed 'Designed by Archibald G. R. Russell, MVO, Lancaster Herald. Drawn by G. Cobb. Made by Cecil Thomas 1938. Arthur John Laker Master'
Thomas Fattorini, Silversmith

SPECIAL REMARKS

In 1892 the Court became aware that there was no Master's Badge and the Clerk reported that a simple one could be made for 10 guineas. The following year the design was approved. The Master selected a motto and the badge displayed the arms originally used by the Woodmongers.

In 1929 the present arms were granted and supporters were added in 1937 when a new badge was commissioned which cost £95. This badge was damaged by fire in the Blitz. The original badge of 1893 is now framed and displayed in the Company's office. The form of frame border used is very similar to that of the Farmers' Master's Badge.

MASTER'S CHAIN

There is a chain

OTHER BADGES

Wardens' Badges are fine examples of silversmiths' craft fashioned in London in silver gilt and hallmarked Goldsmiths' Hall, London. Gift of G.H. Lloyd (Master in 1922 and 1930). There are badges for the Clerk, Past Masters and Court Assistants.

The Honourable Company of
MASTER MARINERS

DESCRIPTION OF MASTER'S BADGE
The badge of 22ct gold is fashioned in the shape of a shield bearing the coat of arms of the Company supported by a mermaid and a merman, with the motto 'Loyalty and Service' within a border of waves and completed by seven large brilliant-cut diamonds symbolising the Seven Seas. Beneath which two cherubs support a pendant mermaid.

DATE OF MANUFACTURE AND DETAILS OF ANY HALLMARKS
1929

NAME OF SILVERSMITH AND DESIGNER
Omar Ramsden
Designed by William Maggs and modelled by A.E. Ulyett assisted by enameller Henri de Konigh

SPECIAL REMARKS
The reverse is inscribed: 'I was wrought by Omar Ramsden for the Honourable Company of Master Mariners by Command of the Right Honourable the Viscount Rothermere PC in the years of our Lord 1929-1930 to commemorate the distinction of H.R.H. The Prince of Wales being the First Master and Sir Burton Chadwick KBE the Founder, being the first Deputy Master'
    The original pattern in repoussé copper is at the Sheffield City Museum.

MASTER'S CHAIN
The collar of 22ct gold depicts marine creatures, mermaids and mermen, inset with rubies, garnets and enamel, culminating with the initials M.M. on a pectin shell.

OTHER BADGES
Immediate Past Master
Past Masters
Clerk
Master's Lady's Badge (work of Peter Knowles-Brown 1975)

The Worshipful Company of
SOLICITORS OF THE CITY OF LONDON

DESCRIPTION OF MASTER'S BADGE

On a shaped 18ct gold oval plate is set a shield with the Company's arms in white and red enamel and gold. The shield is enclosed to left and right by two figures modelled in gold (perhaps Gog and Magog) above which is an upright sword and swags in modelled gold all surmounted by the Company's crest in gold, enamel and silver.

DATE OF MANUFACTURE AND DETAILS OF ANY HALLMARKS

1926

NAME OF SILVERSMITH AND DESIGNER

The badge was presented by 19 members of the Court in 1926 and is probably the work of Toye, Kenning and Spencer.

SPECIAL REMARKS

The Company does not have supporters in their grant of arms, hence the use of allegorical figures in the badge.

MASTER'S CHAIN

In silver gilt (1966) with a centre piece donated by T.G. Bennett (Master 1964/5) and 16 smaller plaques provided by Sir Desmond Heap and his successors as Master.

OTHER BADGES

Wardens' Badges (1976) gifts of G. Hume Mitchell (Master, 1973-4) and the Master Chamberlain (Master 1975-6) replaced badges given in 1958 by E. Bryden Besant that were then converted into badges for the Stewards but were subsequently lost and not replaced.

Clerk's Badge (1970) in silver gilt and enamel was donated by the then Clerk and his predecessors since grant of livery.

Master's Lady's Badge (1988) gift of D.F. Gray

Badge for the Vice President of the City of London Law Society (1986), gift of Sir Max Williams (Master, 1986-7).

The Worshipful Company of
FARMERS

DESCRIPTION OF MASTER'S BADGE

Within a gold circlet with finials at top, bottom, left and right projecting beyond a circlet of red enamel bearing the legend in gold: 'MASTER THE WORSHIPFUL COMPANY OF FARMERS' this encircling a pierced and robust representation of the Company's full achievement in gold and coloured enamels. The design is very similar to that of the Carmen.

DATE OF MANUFACTURE AND DETAILS OF ANY HALLMARKS

1955-6
Full hallmarks for London 18ct and year letter S and LGD

NAME OF SILVERSMITH AND DESIGNER

Leslie G. Durbin

SPECIAL REMARKS

Three 18ct gold badges with enamelling, depicting the Company's coat of arms, designed with advice from the College of Arms, were commissioned for use by the Master and Wardens in 1955.

MASTER'S CHAIN

The chain embodies 27 hallmarked silver gilt links, the central one portraying the arms of the City from which the Master's Badge is suspended. The remaining 26 scallop-shaped links are each surmounted by a circular hand-painted enamel illustrating, either literally or allegorically, the progress and history of British Agriculture. It was the gift of PM Herbert Graves in 1971.

OTHER BADGES

Wardens (1955) in 18ct gold
Past Masters
Clerk (Toye, Kenning & Spencer, Birmingham 1997) – the gift of W.M. Cornish, Master 1996-7

The Guild of
AIR PILOTS AND AIR NAVIGATORS

DESCRIPTION OF MASTER'S BADGE

The original unofficial arms adopted in the 1930s are shown in enamel on a circle set on an elaborate gold background engraved at the foot with legend 'FOUNDED 1929' over which is a gold and blue enamel scroll with the motto 'WE FLY'. Above the shield is a similar gold and blue scroll bearing the words 'THE GUILD OF AIR PILOTS'. At the top of the badge is a gold and enamel representation of St George slaying the dragon.

DATE OF MANUFACTURE AND DETAILS OF ANY HALLMARKS

1936

NAME OF SILVERSMITH AND DESIGNER

[Perhaps] Fattorini

SPECIAL REMARKS

At a Reception at Mansion House on 12 October 1936 the Duke of Kent (Grand Master) presented the Master's Badge to Captain Guest. On the reverse of the badge is the inscription 'The Gift of W. Austin Balls, OBE, presented by HRH The Duke of Kent, KG, KT, GCMG, GCVO October 12th 1936'.

Official arms were granted by the College of Arms in 1956 – unlike many such 'regularisations' of unofficial arms in this case the College devised a completely different shield and the motto, which had caused some contention in the 1930s was replaced with the more impressive 'PER CAELUM VIA NOSTRA'. The new shield is embodied in the chain.

MASTER'S CHAIN

21 decorated gold shields each linked by two gold chains with – on each shoulder – a winged gold plaque each set with an enamel representation of the official shield of the Company's arms.

OTHER BADGES

Grand Master – This badge, and the Master's, are the original badges of Office owned by the Guild.
Patron
Warden
Clerk
Court Assistants
All badges (except Grand Master and Master) show the full achievement of the Guild's official arms.

The Worshipful Company of
TOBACCO PIPE MAKERS

DESCRIPTION OF MASTER'S BADGE

On a gold shield with a raised border is shown the arms of the Company in raised relief in gold, silver and enamel and in base the shield, crest and mantling of the City of London. Above the shield is shown two sailing ships on stylised waves on either side of a globe of the world surmounted by three stylised leaves in outline all in gold.

DATE OF MANUFACTURE AND DETAILS OF ANY HALLMARKS

1962 (replacing earlier badge)
Fully hallmarked

NAME OF SILVERSMITH AND DESIGNER

Crafted by Norman Bassant

SPECIAL REMARKS

A badge was made when the Company reformed in 1952, and this was mislaid. The current badge commissioned in 1962 is the gift of the Master R.J. Freeman, OBE, VRD. This information is engraved upon the reverse.

MASTER'S CHAIN

Composed of alternate links depicting twisted tobacco leaves and roundels engraved with initials of the Company's name.

OTHER BADGES

Wardens (presented by Alfred H. Dunhill 1957)
Clerk
Mistress's Jewel
Treasurer/Assistant Clerk

The Worshipful Company of
FURNITURE MAKERS

DESCRIPTION OF MASTER'S BADGE
The Company's armorial bearings are shown in rich enamels and silver within an oval blue enamel and gilt border bearing the legend THE FURNITURE MAKERS COMPANY MASTER. There are four decorative finials to the top, bottom and left and right of the oval.

DATE OF MANUFACTURE AND DETAILS OF ANY HALLMARKS
1954
Full hallmarks with date letter T and LGD

NAME OF SILVERSMITH AND DESIGNER
Leslie G. Durbin

SPECIAL REMARKS
Presented by Sir Herman Lebus, CBE, JP (Master 1954-5). The reverse is engraved with the full achievement of Sir Herman's arms and the inscription commemorating his gift of the badge.

MASTER'S CHAIN
A double silver chain linking 11 three-sectioned silver scrolls and at the base a representation of the full achievement of the City's arms in silver and white and red enamels from which can be suspended the Master's Badge. All set on a blue ribbon.

OTHER BADGES
Senior Warden's and Junior Wardens' Badges in silver gilt and enamel were presented by Ald. Sir Ralph E. Perring, Bt to commemorate his year as Sheriff (1958-9). The Clerk's Badge in silver gilt presented by John S. Allpreiss, MC (Master 1965-6)

The Worshipful Company of
SCIENTIFIC INSTRUMENT MAKERS

DESCRIPTION OF MASTER'S BADGE

The Company's shield of arms in yellow gold, blue sapphire and white gold with the charges worked in gold, silver and onyx is surmounted by a helmet in silver and the crest in 18ct gold and flanked by the supporters of chased gold and coloured enamels. The achievement is mounted on a white gold background which is surrounded by a free standing frame of diamonds, yellow sapphires and onyx, connected by eight oval pointed Montana sapphires.

DATE OF MANUFACTURE AND DETAILS OF ANY HALLMARKS

1959

NAME OF SILVERSMITH AND DESIGNER

Designed and made by Francis J.C. Cooper at Westminster

SPECIAL REMARKS

MASTER'S CHAIN

Enamelled collar depicting scientific instruments of historic importance

OTHER BADGES

Wardens
Clerk

The Worshipful Company of
CHARTERED SURVEYORS

DESCRIPTION OF MASTER'S BADGE
The full achievement of the Company in pierced gold and coloured enamels.
There is another version where the achievement sits within a dished oval set within three circles of overlapping
petals all in gold, used as the Master's Travelling Badge.

DATE OF MANUFACTURE AND DETAILS OF ANY HALLMARKS
1977 TK&S
Hallmarked

NAME OF SILVERSMITH AND DESIGNER
Toye Kenning & Spencer

SPECIAL REMARKS
The badge was commissioned by the Court

MASTER'S CHAIN
There is a chain of two strands of gold linking a number of gold discs

OTHER BADGES
Master's Travelling Badge (see above), the work of Grant Macdonald
Senior Warden
Junior Warden
Court Assistants
Past Masters
Honorary Chaplain
Clerk

The Worshipful Company of
CHARTERED ACCOUNTANTS

DESCRIPTION OF MASTER'S BADGE

The Company's arms in relief, with the shield in blue enamel, on a disc and set within a raised circlet bearing the legend 'THE WORSHIPFUL COMPANY OF CHARTERED ACCOUNTANTS MASTER' all surrounded by an elaborate border with cruciform extensions all in silver gilt.

DATE OF MANUFACTURE AND DETAILS OF ANY HALLMARKS

1978

NAME OF SILVERSMITH AND DESIGNER

Aspreys

SPECIAL REMARKS

During 1978 instructions were given to Messrs Aspreys to design and manufacture jewels of office for the Master, Wardens and Court Assistants.
In October 2011 the Court agreed on the design of a new badge for the Master (see p.13)

MASTER'S CHAIN

A double chain inset with scrolls capable of being engraved with the names of Masters

OTHER BADGES

Wardens
Court Assistants
Clerk

The Worshipful Company of
CHARTERED SECRETARIES AND ADMINISTRATORS

DESCRIPTION OF MASTER'S BADGE

Set within a silver dished circle a shield of blue enamelled silver showing the Company's arms in coloured enamels. The inner surface of the dished roundel has a matt silver finish with radiating striations. The outer lip of the roundel is polished and bears the inscription THE WORSHIPFUL COMPANY OF CHARTERED SECRETARIES AND ADMINISTRATORS and SERVICE WITH INTEGRITY

DATE OF MANUFACTURE AND DETAILS OF ANY HALLMARKS

1982

NAME OF SILVERSMITH AND DESIGNER

Designed by J.M. Willmin. Made by Toye, Kenning & Spencer

SPECIAL REMARKS

First worn by Mr D.C.L. Marwood at the Livery Dinner held at the Mansion House on 19 March 1982
The badge measures four inches in diameter and weighs four ounces

MASTER'S CHAIN

The Master's Badge is worn from a collar when the Master is robed or from a blue ribbon or gold chain otherwise

OTHER BADGES

Master's Lady
Wardens (2 identical badges)
Past Masters
Clerk
Assistant Clerk
Hon. Chaplain
Court Assistants wear a blue ribbon with a metal bar saying 'Court Assistant' – not a proper badge
There is also a similar ribbon with a bar saying 'For meritorious service' - only two in issue to date

The Worshipful Company of
BUILDERS MERCHANTS

DESCRIPTION OF MASTER'S BADGE
The Company's full achievement of arms in silver gilt, silver and enamels is set upon an open pierced oval frame bearing the word MASTER on a pierced scroll above the arms.

DATE OF MANUFACTURE AND DETAILS OF ANY HALLMARKS
Hallmarked

NAME OF SILVERSMITH AND DESIGNER

SPECIAL REMARKS
The depiction of the Company's arms follows very closely the illustration on the Letters Patent of the grant of arms.

MASTER'S CHAIN
Comprising gold roundels set within a pierced border and joined by a double linked chain

OTHER BADGES
Senior and Junior Wardens
Master's Lady
Past Masters
Past Masters' Ladies
Clerk

The Worshipful Company of
LAUNDERERS

DESCRIPTION OF MASTER'S BADGE

Oval (115mm x 90mm) yellow gold (stamped 9ct).

The centre applied with gold and enamelled coat of arms; the base with applied leaves and scroll motif; outer border decorated with raised scrolls and beads.

Obverse:

Hollow oval applied back.

Hand engraved:

The gift of Stanley Walter Wells MBE CC Master 1959-1961

DATE OF MANUFACTURE AND DETAILS OF ANY HALLMARKS

1963/64

NAME OF SILVERSMITH AND DESIGNER

Mr Phillips of Hicklenton & Phillips is quoted but that company was not a manufacturer and would have sub-contracted the work.

SPECIAL REMARKS

The gift of Stanley Walter Wells MBE CC Master, 1959-61

MASTER'S CHAIN

Length: 91.5cm

Sterling silver 20 oval pierced edged links (each section 40mm x 25mm) each oval *link separated by 3x3 links (*pattern link W838/TF Design Ref BO30401-04)

Joining rings for jewel. Hard gold plated

Weight: 248 grams

Maker: Thomas Fattorini Ltd, Birmingham; June 2003

OTHER BADGES

1969 Senior Warden's & Renter Warden's and Past Masters' Badges

1973 Clerk's Badge

The Worshipful Company of
MARKETORS

DESCRIPTION OF MASTER'S BADGE

Within an open gold frame is depicted the full arms of the Company in gold and various coloured enamels. Beneath the achievement is shown on a scroll the title WORSHIPFUL COMPANY OF MARKETORS

DATE OF MANUFACTURE AND DETAILS OF ANY HALLMARKS

Hallmarked Birmingham, TKS and indistinct year letter but probably 1977

NAME OF SILVERSMITH AND DESIGNER

Toye, Kenning & Spencer

SPECIAL REMARKS

The Master's Badge was presented by the Institute of Marketing (later the Chartered Institute) from whom the founding members were all drawn

MASTER'S CHAIN

The chain contains links upon which are engraved the names of all Past Masters.

OTHER BADGES

Founder Master's Badge (presented by Roy Randolph in 1977)
3 Wardens' Badges – the gift of an anonymous donor
Master's Lady's Badge was presented by Mrs Joe Bellm, wife of the second Master
Clerk's Badge – the gift of Mr T. Foley
Past Masters

The Worshipful Company of
ACTUARIES

DESCRIPTION OF MASTER'S BADGE

Perhaps one of the most original of all badges in concept and design, the Badge is in the shape of a three dimensional (albeit the rear is flat to sit more comfortably when worn and the badge hollow to reduce the weight) hour glass in silver with the Company's arms placed centrally on the narrowed neck of the hourglass with the supporters between the 'wings' of the hour glass all in gold. On the upper face of the badge are engraved various mathematical symbols associated with actuarial calculations.

DATE OF MANUFACTURE AND DETAILS OF ANY HALLMARKS

2008 (replacing an earlier badge of 1980)

NAME OF SILVERSMITH AND DESIGNER

Grant Macdonald

In order to create the current badge Grant Macdonald had first to make a wooden pattern

SPECIAL REMARKS

In January 1980 it was agreed that the founder members of the Court should pay for their own robes, jewels and collar. The Founder Master, Geoffrey Heywood, had the Master's Badge made on Merseyside. In later years, having commissioned various items of silver, including a loving cup, from Grant Macdonald, the Company decided to commission a new badge for the Master. This was received in 2008 and was the gift of the Master of the day. The present badge is therefore engraved on the reverse 'Chris Ide Master 2007-2008'. The original badge is now worn by the Immediate Past Master.

MASTER'S CHAIN

The Master's chain is made up of a series of crosses potent linked by gold chain

OTHER BADGES

The Wardens, Court Assistants, Clerk and Past Masters all have badges, being a two dimensional looped replication of the Master's Badge.

The Worshipful Company of
INSURERS

DESCRIPTION OF MASTER'S BADGE

An oval silver gilt medallion with a decorated pierced border within which is an enamel plaque bearing the legend THE WORSHIPFUL COMPANY OF INSURERS in gilt letters on a red enamel border surrounding a white enamel oval on which is depicted the Company's armorial bearings.

DATE OF MANUFACTURE AND DETAILS OF ANY HALLMARKS

1981
Hallmarks somewhat indistinct

NAME OF SILVERSMITH AND DESIGNER

SPECIAL REMARKS

The Master's Badge and the badges of the Senior and Junior Wardens were presented by the Corporation of Lloyds and the Master's Badge bears on the reverse the inscription: 'Presented to the Company by the Committee of Lloyds London 15th January 1981'. Despite this date there is reference elsewhere that it was first worn at the Company's first livery dinner held at Mansion House on 28 April 1980.

MASTER'S CHAIN

The Master's Chain of Office was the personal gift of the Founder Master Bill Harris. Designed in 1982 by the jeweller Lexi Dick.

OTHER BADGES

Wardens
Clerk

The Worshipful Company of
ARBITRATORS

DESCRIPTION OF MASTER'S BADGE

The Company's full achievement of arms in silver gilt and various enamels (red, green, white and black) set on a pierced and beaded octofoil in gold.

DATE OF MANUFACTURE AND DETAILS OF ANY HALLMARKS

2001 (replacing the original of 1982)

NAME OF SILVERSMITH AND DESIGNER

Hallmarked silver gilt and enamel designed and made by Toye Kenning & Spencer in September 2001

SPECIAL REMARKS

In 1982 the Court agreed that a badge should be ordered for the Master at a cost of around £1,100 + VAT. The Master proposed to make a substantial contribution and the Wardens were also prepared to contribute.

In June 1982 the badge was first displayed but later it was considered too small and not in general keeping with all other Masters' Badges and in 2001 a new badge was presented by Victoria Russell and Michael Wilkey. The original badge was re-designated the Senior Past Master's Badge and is now (2011) being reassigned to either the Immediate Past or Deputy Master.

MASTER'S CHAIN

Made by Toye, Keening & Spencer in September 2001 in hallmarked silver gilt to accompany the new badge and presented to the Company by Victoria Russell and M.D.J. Wilkey.

OTHER BADGES

In 1984 Wardens' and Past Masters' Badges were ordered but in 2001 new Wardens' and Clerk's Badges were made to match the new badge for the Master.

Court Assistants Badges and livery medals exist.

The Worshipful Company of
ENGINEERS

DESCRIPTION OF MASTER'S BADGE
A fine representation of the Company's arms in pierced 9ct gold and vitreous enamel work, surmounted by the achievement of the City in gold and enamels.

DATE OF MANUFACTURE AND DETAILS OF ANY HALLMARKS
1983
TKS

NAME OF SILVERSMITH AND DESIGNER
Toye, Kenning & Spencer

SPECIAL REMARKS

MASTER'S CHAIN
Made in 1983 from 9ct gold. The links are engraved with the names of Past Masters.

OTHER BADGES
Master's Travelling Badge presented in November 1995 by Mr L.F. Turner, OBE (Master 1995-6). Made in 9ct gold by Alan Henn of T.A. Henn & Son Ltd, Wolverhampton.
3 Warden's Badges (1983 silver gilt by Toye, Kenning & Spencer)
Past Master's Badges (1983 [onwards] silver gilt by Toye, Kenning & Spencer)
Clerk (1983 in rhodium plated silver by Toye, Kenning & Spencer)
Assistant Clerk (1993 in rhodium plated silver by Toye, Kenning & Spencer)
Court Assistants' (1995, 1997 silver by Toye, Kenning & Spencer)
Court Assistants' Badges

The Worshipful Company of
FUELLERS

Description of Master's Badge

Standing on a scroll bearing the motto the Company's supporters all in gold hold the Company's shield in silver and coloured enamels surmounted by the helm, mantling and crest in silver and gold all held within a gold 'teardrop shaped' frame.

Date of Manufacture and Details of any Hallmarks

1983

Name of Silversmith and Designer

Special Remarks

Master's Badge presented by Charles E. Needham, C.B.E. on 28 October 1983

Master's Chain

Presented by Past Master Brian Harrison, CBE

Other Badges

Senior and Junior Wardens' Badges presented by Founder Master (Charles Stephenson Clarke). His wife, Therese, presented a Master's Lady's Badge though this is now worn by the Senior Lady Warden. The current Master's Lady's Jewel was presented by Past Master Bainbridge, his wife and Past Master Pybus.

The Worshipful Company of
LIGHTMONGERS

DESCRIPTION OF MASTER'S BADGE
The full achievement of arms in gold, silver and coloured enamels is set within a dished gold oval surmounted by a scroll the centre section of which bears the word MASTER in gold on red enamel.

DATE OF MANUFACTURE AND DETAILS OF ANY HALLMARKS
1983
Hallmarked

NAME OF SILVERSMITH AND DESIGNER
Hallmarked (perhaps) T.D.

SPECIAL REMARKS
On 25 February 1983 the Board of Directors of ASEE Exhibitions Ltd wished to make a financial donation to provide for the purchase of a Master's Jewel.

The badge is engraved on the reverse 'Presented by Electrex November 1983'.

In November the Court approved expenditure for the purchase of jewels for the Wardens and Clerk.

MASTER'S CHAIN
Gold linked chain, gift of Liveryman John Inglis

OTHER BADGES
Wardens
Clerk

The Worshipful Company of
ENVIRONMENTAL CLEANERS

DESCRIPTION OF MASTER'S BADGE

The Company's arms painted on a white enamel circle surrounded by a blue border bearing the legend 'THE WORSHIPFUL COMPANY OF ENVIRONMENTAL CLEANERS' all enclosed within an ornamental border in gold of leaves and flowers. At the top a gold shield depicting the City arms in rubies and diamonds.

DATE OF MANUFACTURE AND DETAILS OF ANY HALLMARKS

1993 (possibly replacing an earlier version)

NAME OF SILVERSMITH AND DESIGNER

SPECIAL REMARKS

It is recorded that in 1993 Deputy Master George Newell presented a splendid new Master's Badge

MASTER'S CHAIN

20 gold ovals (some) bear the names of two Masters each joined by two links of gold chain to its neighbour and terminating in an elaborately bordered oval with a hook to take the badge.

OTHER BADGES

Senior Warden
Junior Warden
Deputy Master
Past Masters
Clerk

The Worshipful Company of
CHARTERED ARCHITECTS

DESCRIPTION OF MASTER'S BADGE

The arms of the Company in gold and red enamel on a roundel set within a circlet of alternate red enamel and gold and surrounded by a golden ring engraved with the legend 'THE COMPANY OF CHARTERED ARCHITECTS MASTER' all surmounted by the Company's crest worked in the round in gold.

DATE OF MANUFACTURE AND DETAILS OF ANY HALLMARKS

1988

NAME OF SILVERSMITH AND DESIGNER

Designed by Sylvia and John Reid and made by George Lukes (London)

SPECIAL REMARKS

John Reid OBE was founder Master and Pageant Master of the City Corporation

MASTER'S CHAIN

Silver chain made by George Lukes and designed by John Reid, and presented in 1988, consisting of a series of plates engraved with the names of Masters on one side and a ridged surface on the other.

OTHER BADGES

Upper Warden
Renter Warden } all dated 1988
Junior Warden
Clerk
Clerk to the Trustees donated in 2005
Deputy Master donated in 2001
Master's Consort donated in 2003

The Worshipful Company of
CONSTRUCTORS

DESCRIPTION OF MASTER'S BADGE

On a square panel with a matt ground are applied the title 'MASTER' and the Company's achievement in coloured enamels and white gold surmounted by a loop above and a black enamel tapered terminal with ruby cabochon below.

DATE OF MANUFACTURE AND DETAILS OF ANY HALLMARKS

1990 Birmingham (full assay marks)

240 grams

NAME OF SILVERSMITH AND DESIGNER

Made by T. Fattorini and designed by David Tong

SPECIAL REMARKS

Engraved on the reverse 'Presented by Geoffrey Prefect, Esq., JP, Master 1989'

An original 'jewel' for the Master of the Guild of Builders was created in 1976

MASTER'S CHAIN

9ct yellow gold triple strand curb link chain with two panels chased with the Company's arms and five tapering panels centred by black onyx cabochons, the central panel containing an enamel plaque inscribed 'THE WORSHIPFUL COMPANY OF CONSTRUCTORS' (Fattorini 1980).

OTHER BADGES

Wardens

Clerk

Past Masters

The Worshipful Company of
INFORMATION TECHNOLOGISTS

DESCRIPTION OF MASTER'S BADGE
On a white enamelled silver oval is depicted a painted representation of the Company's achievement in full colour. This is set within an open silver border bearing at its head a scroll with the inscription MASTER and at the foot a scroll bearing THE COMPANY OF INFORMATION TECHNOLOGISTS, both in blue enamel on white background.

DATE OF MANUFACTURE AND DETAILS OF ANY HALLMARKS
JWB

NAME OF SILVERSMITH AND DESIGNER

SPECIAL REMARKS

MASTER'S CHAIN
There is a chain

OTHER BADGES
Wardens
Clerk
Past Masters

The Worshipful Company of
WORLD TRADERS

DESCRIPTION OF MASTER'S BADGE

On a base of rock crystal carved with an outline of the globe showing the five continents set within a ribbed wheel of five spokes all of gold is depicted the full achievement of the Company's arms wrought in gold and enamel all in high relief.

DATE OF MANUFACTURE AND DETAILS OF ANY HALLMARKS

1991 Full hallmarks [date letter R]

NAME OF SILVERSMITH AND DESIGNER

Hallmark for SJC

SPECIAL REMARKS

A competition was held in 1991 to design the Master's Badge and was first worn by Brian Whalley as Master. The piece of rock crystal upon which the Company's arms are engraved was donated by the World Trade Centre of Rio de Janeiro.

The reverse is engraved 'Guild of World Traders Master's Badge Established 1985' together with a facsimile signature (difficult to decipher).

MASTER'S CHAIN

Full Jubilee hallmark, BMBC date letter for 2002. The chain is made up of seven hand-painted sterling silver coloured plaques: Accountancy and Law, shown by an abacus and the figure of justice; Banking and Insurance shown by a purse, coinage and the sun face; Oil and Pharmaceuticals shown by an oil rig and apothecary's jar; Farming and Food shown by a sheaf of wheat and a load of bread; Air and Sea Transport shown by Concorde and a container ship; Theatre and Education shown by theatrical masks and a mortar board; Construction and Armaments shown by a brick, trowel and cannon.

These are linked between by badges bearing features taken from the Master's Jewel. Five purses representing trade with the five continents. The medieval merchant's cap; and within the wheel of St Catherine the company coat of arms and compass.

The Master's Badge of Office is suspended from the centre hand-painted plaque representing Oil and Pharmaceuticals showing the association with Past Master Hughes whose initial idea it was, during her year as Master, to provide a Chain of Office for the Master.

OTHER BADGES

Wardens, Past Masters, Court Assistants, Clerk, all with full hallmarks for 2002 and BMBC.

Master's Consort's Jewel – hallmarked BMBC and date letter for 2003 engraved on reverse 'Presented by John L. Stace, Master 2002-2003'.

The Worshipful Company of
WATER CONSERVATORS

DESCRIPTION OF MASTER'S BADGE
On a gold oval is set a white enamel oval painted with the full achievement of the Company in colour. This is surmounted by a blue enamel plaque bearing the legend MASTER in gold. Beneath the achievement is another scroll of blue enamel bearing the words THE WORSHIPFUL COMPANY OF WATER CONSERVATORS. Around the border between the two scrolls are 11 depictions of the 'tear drop' motif. This image was created by Salvador Dali.

DATE OF MANUFACTURE AND DETAILS OF ANY HALLMARKS
1984 Hallmarked Birmingham

NAME OF SILVERSMITH AND DESIGNER
Thomas Fattorini

SPECIAL REMARKS
On 28 September 1984 the Master and Assistant Clerk reported that a very competitive quotation and design for the Master's and Clerk's Badges had been received from Fattorini. These were £2,875 + VAT and £875 + VAT respectively, both for 9ct gold. The title 'Company of Water Conservators' on the Master's Badge could be removed and 'Worshipful Company' substituted at the appropriate time. The designs were accepted and a fine of £250 from each Court Member as agreed previously had been collected.

MASTER'S CHAIN
A collar of Gold Tear Drops, presented to the Company by Past Master Ted Flaxman

OTHER BADGES
Past Master's Badges (the gift of Past Master McDowell)
Wardens' (Thames, Fleet & Walbrook) Badges
Clerk

The Worshipful Company of
FIREFIGHTERS

DESCRIPTION OF MASTER'S BADGE

Within a dished and decorated gold border incised with radiating lines, headed by a panel with the word 'MASTER' in black enamel, is a white enamel disc fired with the painted achievement of the Company in full colour.

DATE OF MANUFACTURE AND DETAILS OF ANY HALLMARKS

1997

NAME OF SILVERSMITH AND DESIGNER

Toye, Kenning and Spencer

SPECIAL REMARKS

MASTER'S CHAIN

A chain was presented to the Company by Colin J. Livett, BEM, Master 2003-4 as a gift from his family. Originally it was a Shrieval chain from Asprey's consisting of three rows of 18ct yellow gold and a multi-coloured enamel coat of arms of the City.

OTHER BADGES

Upper Warden
Under Warden
Renter Warden
Clerk
Past Masters

CUM SCIENTIA SERVIMUS

The Worshipful Company of
HACKNEY CARRIAGE DRIVERS

DESCRIPTION OF MASTER'S BADGE

The full achievement of arms of the Company in pierced gold and enamel

DATE OF MANUFACTURE AND DETAILS OF ANY HALLMARKS

2004
Fully hallmarked

NAME OF SILVERSMITH AND DESIGNER

SPECIAL REMARKS

This Master's Badge replaces an earlier one created before the Company received Livery

MASTER'S CHAIN

There is no chain

OTHER BADGES

Upper Warden
Lower Warden
Renter Warden
Past Masters
Clerk
Hon. Chaplain
Court Assistant

CHANGE THROUGH WISDOM

The Worshipful Company of
MANAGEMENT CONSULTANTS

DESCRIPTION OF MASTER'S BADGE
A representation of the Company's full achievement of arms in pierced gold and red and white enamel work

DATE OF MANUFACTURE AND DETAILS OF ANY HALLMARKS
Hallmarked Birmingham

NAME OF SILVERSMITH AND DESIGNER
Maker's mark possibly JWB

SPECIAL REMARKS

MASTER'S CHAIN
There is a chain

OTHER BADGES
Wardens
Clerk

A·NATIONE·AD·NATIONEM

The Worshipful Company of
INTERNATIONAL BANKERS

Description of Master's Badge
Within a wavy gold frame set on its outer edge with seven golden balls is placed a pierced openwork representation of the Company's achievement in gold, silver and coloured enamels.

Date of Manufacture and Details of any Hallmarks
2004

Name of Silversmith and Designer
John Donald

Special Remarks
Commissioned by the Court

Master's Chain
No chain

Other Badges
3 Wardens
Clerk
Liverymen's Badges

The Worshipful Company of
TAX ADVISERS

DESCRIPTION OF MASTER'S BADGE

A three dimensional representation of a medieval money purse in sterling silver with gold-plated coins 'tumbling' from the opening and down the left-hand side of the purse. To the right hand is a representation of the cord and tassels in gold whilst in the centre is set the hand carved coat of arms of the Company in gold-plated silver The purse of charitable provision is taken from the Company's crest where it is shown held by an owl.

DATE OF MANUFACTURE AND DETAILS OF ANY HALLMARKS

2006

NAME OF SILVERSMITH AND DESIGNER

Grant Macdonald

SPECIAL REMARKS

The Badge replaces an earlier simpler version depicting the Company's coat of arms in enamel on gold produced by Toye, Kenning & Spencer, which is currently on loan to the Museum of London.

MASTER'S CHAIN

Two stranded chain in gold with links representing the shield from the Coat of Arms. Manufactured by Toye, Kenning & Spencer in 2005 [?].

OTHER BADGES

3 Wardens' Badges – sterling silver part gold plated comprising the Company's arms applied to a three strand symbolic shape of a coin purse.

Past Masters' Badges – sterling silver part gold plated comprising the Company's arms applied to a two strand symbolic shape of a coin purse.

Court Assistants – sterling silver part gold plated comprising the Company's arms applied to a single strand symbolic shape of a coin purse.

Clerk, Assistant Clerk and Chaplain's Badges: as Court Assistants but with a small pair of gold crossed quills, gold quill or silver cross on ribbon to denote office.

All manufactured by Grant Macdonald (2006).

The Worshipful Company of
SECURITY PROFESSIONALS

DESCRIPTION OF MASTER'S BADGE

Set within a pierced three-dimensional portcullis in silver gilt formed into a bowl-shape, giving an intriguing three-dimensional feel, is the full achievement of the Company's arms in gold and painted enamels.

DATE OF MANUFACTURE AND DETAILS OF ANY HALLMARKS

February 2008

NAME OF SILVERSMITH AND DESIGNER

Grant Macdonald

SPECIAL REMARKS

On becoming a Company without Livery in 2004, a Livery Celebration Fund was established from which – among other things – the robes and regalia could be purchased. In 2007 Grand Macdonald was commissioned to create the Master's Badge along with the badges for the Immediate Past Master, Wardens, Clerk and Treasurer. Only the Master's Badge was ready, a few days before 2 May 2008, just in time for the presentation of the Letters Patent of the Livery Grant at Mansion House. The original plan was to have the Master's Badge studded with diamonds (but this awaits the generosity of a future benefactor!) Subsequently, badges were commissioned for Past Masters and the Master's Consort.

MASTER'S CHAIN

There is no chain

OTHER BADGES

Senior Warden
Warden
Immediate Past Master
Chaplain
Clerk
Treasurer
Past Masters
Master's Consort

The Worshipful Company of
PARISH CLERKS

DESCRIPTION OF MASTER'S BADGE

The shield of the Company's arms in silver parcel gilt, jewels and blue and red enamel interspersed with golden dots surmounted by a helm. To either side are representations in gilt and silver of the Company's supporters standing on a motto scroll whilst above the helm is the crest, also gilded.

DATE OF MANUFACTURE AND DETAILS OF ANY HALLMARKS

1990 replacing original of 1878. Fully hallmarked with maker's mark: BMW

NAME OF SILVERSMITH AND DESIGNER

Barry Witmond, silversmith of Burleigh, Stamford, Lincs.

SPECIAL REMARKS

The badge was the gift of John Gaze, Master 1990 in memory of Sir Edward Cooper, Parish Clerk and Lord Mayor 1921.

The original badge was the gift of Richard Perkins in 1879 and bears the inscription, 'Hoc insigne in usum magistri d[ono] d[edit] Richardus Perkins, S.S. Augustini et Fidei clericus'. It is now used as a Travelling Badge by the Master.

MASTER'S CHAIN

Comprising triple chains of silver gilt terminating in two enamels bearing the full arms of the City from one of which the Master's Badge is pendant. This was the shrieval chain of Alan Seymour Lambert, Past Master and former Sheriff.

OTHER BADGES

Wardens' Badges
Past Masters
Clerk
The Master's former badge now used as the Travelling Badge [see above]

The Worshipful Company of
WATERMEN AND LIGHTERMEN

DESCRIPTION OF MASTER'S BADGE

On a shaped and tapered rectangular gold plate are set two heavily modelled spirited dolphin supporters in gold between which is a fine enamel shield of the Company's arms surmounted by a torse and the Company's crest modelled in gold. Below the shield of arms is another shield in gold inscribed 1514 (date of the first Act of Parliament to control Watermen) and above a scroll bearing the motto AT COMAVNDE OF OVR SVPERIOVRS. Around the badge is entwined a gold rope.

DATE OF MANUFACTURE AND DETAILS OF ANY HALLMARKS

1878

NAME OF SILVERSMITH AND DESIGNER

Messrs. Brown & Co.

SPECIAL REMARKS

In 1878 the subject of a distinguishing badge or jewel to be worn by the Master for the time being was considered by the Court and referred to the Committee for further consideration and enquiry as to cost, etc. Later the Court approved the design of Messrs Brown and Co., the costs to be paid by subscription of the Members of the Court and the Company.

MASTER'S CHAIN

Made of open rectangular plates of gold containing three wavy bars alternately charged with crossed oars and a dolphin all linked by double gold chains. On the reverse of a solid plate is engraved 'Presented to the Company of Watermen & Lightermen of the River Thames by Percival E.T. Johnson a Freeman in memory of John Michael Price Member of the Court of the Company 1888-1912-1937'.

OTHER BADGES

Deputy Master (presented by Harry H. Higgs 1938)
Senior Warden
Junior Wardens (3)
The Clerk
The Chaplain
Past Masters

Appendix I

SCHEDULE OF DATES OF MASTERS' BADGES

First badge	Name of Company	Current badge
pre-1750	The Worshipful Company of Vintners	1878
1772	The Worshipful Company of Pattenmakers	Not known
perhaps 1789	The Worshipful Company of Innholders	1879
1800	The Worshipful Company of Needlemakers	1986
1841	The Worshipful Company of Clothworkers	1905
1852	The Worshipful Company of Distillers	1852
c1854	The Worshipful Company of Dyers	1854
1857	The Worshipful Company of Merchant Taylors	1857
1861	The Worshipful Company of Fishmongers	1877
1865	The Worshipful Company of Fruiterers	1955
1868	The Worshipful Company of Saddlers	1868
1869	The Worshipful Company of Spectacle Makers	1991
1870	The Worshipful Company of Blacksmiths	1870
1871	The Worshipful Company of Mercers	1871
1871	The Worshipful Company of Carpenters	1933
1871	The Worshipful Company of Leathersellers	1934
1871	The Worshipful Company of Pewterers	1871
1872	The Worshipful Company of Cooks	1872
1872	The Worshipful Company of Coopers	1872
1872	The Worshipful Company of Plaisterers	1872
1873	The Worshipful Company of Clockmakers	1924
1873	The Worshipful Company of Masons	1973
1873	The Worshipful Company of Wheelwrights	1873
1874	The Worshipful Company of Broderers	1874
1874	The Worshipful Company of Butchers	1986
1874	The Worshipful Company of Farriers	1874
1874	The Worshipful Company of Glass Sellers	1922
1874	The Worshipful Company of Ironmongers	1874
1874	The Worshipful Company of Skinners	1874
1875	The Worshipful Company of Armourers and Brasiers	1875
1875	The Worshipful Company of Bakers	1912
1875	The Worshipful Company of Glaziers & Painters of Glass	1900
1875	The Worshipful Company of Haberdashers	1875
1876	The Worshipful Company of Plumbers	1887
1876	The Worshipful Company of Shipwrights	1876
1876	The Worshipful Company of Upholders	2000
1877	The Worshipful Company of Barbers	1877
1877	The Worshipful Company of Turners	1877
1878	The Worshipful Company of Fan Makers	1878
1878	The Worshipful Company of Gunmakers	1878
1878	The Worshipful Company of Stationers and Newspaper Makers	1878

1878	The Company of Watermen & Lightermen	1878
1878	The Worshipful Company of Weavers	1878
1878	The Worshipful Company of Parish Clerks	1990
1879	The Worshipful Company of Fletchers	1899
1879	The Worshipful Company of Musicians	1879
1879	The Worshipful Company of Poulters	1879
1879	The Worshipful Company of Scriveners	1879
1880	The Worshipful Company of Wax Chandlers	Victorian
1880	The Worshipful Company of Cutlers	1880
1880	The Worshipful Company of Girdlers	1950
1880	The Worshipful Company of Gold and Silver Wyre Drawers	1880
1880	The Worshipful Company of Horners	1992
1880	The Worshipful Company of Makers of Playing Cards	1951
1880	The Worshipful Company of Woolmen	1964
1881	The Worshipful Company of Framework Knitters	1881
1881	The Worshipful Company of Painter-Stainers	1881
1882	The Worshipful Company of Drapers	1882
1883	The Worshipful Company of Tallow Chandlers	1963
1884	The Worshipful Company of Bowyers	1996
1884	The Worshipful Company of Curriers	1884
1886	The Worshipful Company of Basketmakers	1916
1887	The Worshipful Company of Salters	1887
1889	The Worshipful Company of Paviors	1942
c.1890	The Worshipful Company of Tylers and Bricklayers	1890
1891	The Worshipful Company of Cordwainers	1891
1892	The Worshipful Company of Feltmakers	1892
1892	The Worshipful Company of Gardeners	1892
1893	The Worshipful Company of Carmen	1938
1900	The Worshipful Company of Brewers	1900
1917	The Worshipful Company of Coachmakers	1917
1919	The Worshipful Society of Apothecaries	1987
Not known	The Worshipful Company of Founders	1924
1926	The Worshipful Company of Solicitors	1926
1929	The Honourable Company of Master Mariners	1929
1936	The Guild of Air Pilots and Air Navigators	1936
1948	The Worshipful Company of Goldsmiths	1953
1952	The Worshipful Company of Tobacco Pipe Makers and Tobacco Blenders	1962
1954	The Worshipful Company of Furniture Makers	1954
1955	The Worshipful Company of Farmers	1955
1959	The Worshipful Company of Scientific Instrument Makers	1959
1963	The Worshipful Company of Launderers	1963
1970	The Worshipful Company of Grocers	1970
Not known	The Worshipful Company of Tin Plate Workers	1970
1977	The Worshipful Company of Marketors	1977
1977	The Worshipful Company of Chartered Surveyors	1977
1978	The Worshipful Company of Chartered Accountants	1978
1980	The Worshipful Company of Actuaries	2008
1981	The Worshipful Company of Insurers	1981
1982	The Worshipful Company of Arbitrators	2001
1982	The Worshipful Company of Chartered Secretaries	1982
1983	The Worshipful Company of Engineers	1983
1983	The Worshipful Company of Fuellers	1983
1983	The Worshipful Company of Lightmongers	1983
1984	The Worshipful Company of Water Conservators	1984
1988	The Worshipful Company of Chartered Architects	1988
1990	The Worshipful Company of Constructors	1990
Not known	The Worshipful Company of Glovers	1990
Not known	The Worshipful Company of Loriners	1990
1991	The Worshipful Company of World Traders	1991
Not known	The Worshipful Company of Environmental Cleaners	1993
1997	The Worshipful Company of Firefighters	1997
2004	The Worshipful Company of International Bankers	2004
Not known	The Worshipful Company of Hackney Carriage Drivers	2004
Not known	The Worshipful Company of Tax Advisers	2006
2008	The Worshipful Company of Security Professionals	2008

No date information is known about the following badges:
The Worshipful Company of Builders Merchants
The Worshipful Company of Information Technologists
The Worshipful Company of Joiners & Ceilers
The Worshipful Company of Management Consultants

Appendix II

GRANTS OF ARMS TO
LIVERY COMPANIES, POST 1954

AIR PILOTS AND AIR NAVIGATORS

Arms: Per pale Sable and Argent in chief two Wings conjoined and in base a Roundel all counterchanged.

Crest: A demi winged Lion Or holding in the paws an Ancient Lamp Azure inflamed proper.

Supporters: On either side a Falcon wings elevated and addorsed proper Belled Or the dexter charged on the breast with a Sun in splendour Gold the sinister Hooded of the last Plumed Sable and charged on the breast with an Estoile irradiated Argent.

Granted: 28 September 1956

TOBACCO PIPE MAKERS & TOBACCO BLENDERS

Arms: Argent on a Mount Vert in base a Tobacco Plant proper a Bordure Murrey.

Crest: A Hand couped at the wrist holding a Root Briar Pipe all proper.

Supporters: Dexter: A North American Negro. Sinister: A Southern Rhodesian Native both proper.

Granted: 8 November 1956

FURNITURE MAKERS

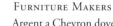

Arms: Argent a Chevron dovetailed counter dovetailed Gules between three Braces and bits palewise with the bit downwards Sable.

Crest: A Cubit Arm the Hand grasping a handplane proper

Granted: 1 October 1954

SCIENTIFIC INSTRUMENT MAKERS

Arms: Tierce in Pairle Azure Or and Argent ten cubes conjoined in perspective four three two and one the tops also Or the dexter and sinister sides Sable and Azure respectively.

Crest: An Antique Bronze Bust of Minerva proper the eyes Argent.

Supporters: Dexter: A figure representing Michael Faraday habited in a Festal Gown of a Doctor of Civil Law of the University of Oxford and holding in the exterior hand a representation of his Coil proper. Sinister: A figure representing Sir Isaac Newton habited in a Gown of a Master of Arts of the University of Cambridge and holding in the exterior hand his Telescope also proper.

Granted: 10 December 1956

Chartered Surveyors

Arms: Sable bezanty a Bar embattled Argent between two barrulets compony Argent and Gules.

Crest: Between two Dragon's wings addorsed Argent an Owl Gules holding in the beak a pair of scales and resting the dexter claw on a garb fesswise Or.

Supporters: On either side a lion guardant Or supporting between the fore legs a Ranging Rod Gules Argent and Sable terminating in the hilt and quillons of a Sword Gules and resting the interior hind paw on a terrestrial globe also Gules the land masses Or that on the dexter side showing the Western and that on the sinister the Eastern Hemisphere.

Granted: 23 April 1979

Chartered Accountants

Arms: Azure three towers checky Argent and Gules the portals Or in that of the first tower the portcullis raised in that of the second tower the portcullis midway and in that of the third tower the portcullis closed Sable out of the battlements of each tower a griffin reguardant Or.

Crest: Between a pair of dragon's wings displayed checky Argent and Gules a cubit arm vested Azure issuing from armour Or the hand proper holding a pair of scales Or.

Supporters: Dexter, a lion Gules head and mane Or gorged with a mural crown checky Argent and Gules and grasping with the sinister forepaw a sword by the blade point upwards Argent with hilt pommel and quillons Gules. Sinister, a dragon Or winged Gules gorged with a like crown and grasping with the dexter foreclaw a key ward upwards and outwards Or.

Granted: 10 April 1979.

Chartered Secretaries and Administrators

Arms: Azure standing on a Book Argent edged Gules and with marker Or a Secretary Bird Or in chief two towers with buttresses Argent masoned Gules.

Crest: A petasus Azure winged Or thereon a lion passant of the last holding in the dexter forepaw a scroll palewise proper with pendant ribbon and seal Gules and tied with ribands also Gules.

Supporters Dexter: A dragon sejent Argent winged Or
Sinister: A Griffin sejent Argent beaked, legged and winged Or each gorged with a wreath Argent and Gules pendant therefrom by a ring a key Or in saltire with a quill pen Azure.

Granted: 6 May 1980

Builders' Merchants

Arms: Azure a representation of a Greek portico comprising five Doric Columns upon a Stylobate with Entablature and Pediment Or a Bordure compony Argent and Gules.

Crest: A Bee volant Or within a voided Hexagon Gules Mantled Gules doubled Argent.

Supporters Dexter: An Owl wings elevated and addorsed Or armed and legged Gules the exterior claw resting on a Log Or

Sinister: A Pelican wings elevated and addorsed Or beaked and legged Gules the exterior foot resting on a Brick Or

Granted: 30 October 1975.

Launderers

Arms: Per pale Or and Argent a representation of Henry Sidgier's mechanical washing machine between three antique flat irons (2 and 1) all proper.

Crest: A white domestic cat cleansing itself within a circlet of lily flowers and sunflowers alternately proper.

Supporters: Dexter, a figure representing Nausicaa robed Purpure draped over the exterior forearm a piece of white sarsenet upon the head a diadem and the interior foot resting upon a washing stone [all proper]. Sinister, a figure representing a laundrymaid of the eighteenth century resting the exterior hand upon a dolly all proper.

Granted: 1 August 1963.

MARKETORS

Arms: Azure a sailing vessel of the reign of Queen Elizabeth I all Or from the masthead a pennant Argent charged with a cross Gules on a chief Or a representation of the Great Beam of London Gules.

Crest: Issuant from a mural crown Argent masoned Gules environed by a chaplet of roses alternately Argent and Gules barbed seeded and leaved Or a cubit arm vested Gules the hand supporting a cornucopia proper.

Supporters: On either side a sea dragon Argent winged Gules on each wing five bezants in cross charged on the breast with a sun in splendour Gules.

Granted: 1 February 1979.

ACTUARIES

Arms: Per chevron checky Argent and Gules and Gules each checker Gules charged with a Bezant and in base a Cross potent Or.

Crest: Three hour glasses in pyramid one upon two the sands of the first discharging from the top thereof those of the second half run out and the sands of the last emptied into the bottom of the glass all proper with the frame Gules.

Supporters: Two winged Sea Dragons Argent their tails Or langued and the inside of the wings fretty Gules each supporting by the outer claw the blade of a Sword erect Gules with the pommel set with a Bezant.

Granted: 15 April 1980.

INSURERS

Arms: Azure a Cross Argent thereon another Gules charged with a pair of Scales Or between in dexter chief and sinister base a Drag Anchor enfiling a Mural Crown and in sinister Chief and dexter base a Salamander Gold in flames proper.

Crest: A Tower Argent masoned Gules with a cruciform window also Gules and having three portals the centremost with portcullis raised Azure in the others a Garb Or and issuing from the battlements two Cubit Arms chevronwise the hands proper holding aloft a Sword with the pommel ringed Gules.

Supporters: Two Lions reguardant Or gorged with a triple Chain Gules, Azure and Vert all from a Ring Gules each resting the interior paw upon a Terrestrial Globe Gold one depicting the land masses of the American Continents and the other those of Europe and Africa proper.

Granted: 3 June 1980.

ARBITRATORS

Arms: Ermine a Chief checky Vert and Or overall a Sword in pale point downwards Gules pendent from the hilt by a ring and surmounting the quillons by its beau a Balance also Gules.

Crest: Out of the top of a Tower Gules masoned Argent a double-headed Lion Gules supporting a torch checky Vert and Or rimmed Gules and enflamed proper.

Supporters: Two dragons Ermine winged Gules, collared checky Vert and Or their forelegs Argent and each supporting by the outer foreleg and angled to the shield a portcullis chained gold. The Compartment comprising a flight of stone steps proper the middle tier incised with the motto: 'Law and Custom'

Granted: 20 April 1983.

ENGINEERS

Arms: Azure on a fess between in chief a Sun in Splendour and in base a Rack and Pinion in profile Or a representation of Tower Bridge London in outline Sable.

Crest: A grassy mount with rocks protruding therefrom proper thereon a representation of Smeaton's Lighthouse (at Plymouth in Devonshire) proper and supporting the same two lions rampant reguardant Gules heads manes and their tails tufted Or and each charged with a mural crown Gules.

Supporters: Dexter, a Pegasus Gules crined winged the tail tufted and hooves Or gorged with a collar and pendent therefrom a sun in splendour also Or thereon a representation of the Iron Bridge (at Ironbridge in Shropshire) proper resting the dexter hoof on a yardstick palewise also proper; sinister, a wyvern erect proper the underwings Or gorged with a collar also Or therefrom a representation of the Jewel of the Lord Mayor of London and resting the sinister claw on a spade palewise proper. In the compartment, in front of water barry wavy of three Azure Argent and Azure a representation of the Iron Bridge (at Ironbridge in Shropshire) proper.

Granted: 28 September 1984.

FUELLERS

Arms: Or between two flaunches Gules thereon each a bunch of faggots proper bound with a tie Sable pierced through with a Sword palewise point upwards Argent hilt pommel and quillons Or a Panther rampant guardant Sable breaking through flames proper and crowned with a Crown rayonny Gules between in chief 2 and in base 1 lozenge Sable.

Crest: Out of a Crown rayonny Gules a Dragon rampant Or wings displayed each per pale Or and Sable and thereon between two barrulets wavy three lozenges counterchanged holding by the fore legs a Collier Brig Sable in full sail pennons flying Gold.

Supporters: Dexter, a carentyne reguardant Sable breathing flames and incensed proper armed crined and tufted and the tail tuft Or gorged with a collar pendent therefrom a chain of three links Gold; sinister, a cockatrice reguardant the tail ending in a dragon's head Sable armed beaked jalloped and wattled Or wings displayed and inverted gorged with a collar pendent therefrom a chain of three links Gold.

Granted: 30 September 1983.

LIGHTMONGERS

Arms: Gules an incandescent flame proper and a chief embattled Argent.

Crest: Issuant from a crown rayonny Gules a dragon Or wings displayed Gules on each a cross moline square pierced also Or and holding an ancient oil lamp enflamed proper.

Supporters: Dexter, a male griffin Purpure étincelé Argent beaked legged rayed and tail tufted Or holding aloft by the inner claws a sun in splendour Gold; sinister, an heraldic panther in train aspect Purpure étincelé Argent incensed proper and holding in the inner paw an increscent moon Argent.

Granted: 24 March 1983.

ENVIRONMENTAL CLEANERS

Arms: Per pale Azure and Argent a Cross couped and in base a spray of Madonna Lilies all counterchanged.

Crest: Issuant from a Mural Crown with five turrets Argent a demi-dragon Azure langued Gules and holding in the fore paws a Besom Brush proper.

Granted: 19 September 1987.

CHARTERED ARCHITECTS

Arms: Gules on a Pavement in perspective a representation of Temple Bar Argent all within a Bordure Argent

Crest: A Column on a pedestal between two Lions statant with their forelegs on the pedestal and guardant all in the manner and being a representation of the Lion Gate at Mycenae Argent.

Granted: 25 November 1988.

CONSTRUCTORS

Arms: Gules a Carpenter's Square in chevron throughout proper surmounted palewise of a T Square Or on a Chief Argent a reinforced concrete Bridge with two main piers spanning Water barry wavy of two Azure and Argent.

Crest: A rainbow and issuant from the inner arc thereof a Cubit Arm the hand holding as if measuring with a Pair of Compasses the points expanded and downwards all proper. Granted to the Company of Builders 26 September 1984; name change to the Company of Constructors on 11 June 1985 recorded at the College.

Information Technologists

Arms: Per pale Vert and Azure a double-warded Key in pale the bow in base and the wards in chief radiated Or amid six Mullets each of six points also radiated Or a chief Gold.

Crest: In a Crown rayonny Or a demi-figure of Mercury Vert purfled Or over his sinister shoulder a Mantle Azure lined Or on his head a Petasus Argent winged Or and his dexter arm raised pointing with the index finger upwards to and supporting at its lowest point a Mullet of six points radiated Gold.

Supporters: Dexter: A Griffin and Sinister: A Horse both gorged with a WreathArgent and Gules and both winged Azure the under-wings Vert and all semy of Mullets of six points irradiated Gold.

Granted: 13 May 1989.

World Traders

Arms: Azure a chief Gules thereon five merchant's purses (3 and 2) each with its drawstrings tassled Or in the Azure its point extending into the Gules a Sword in pale the quillons set with a wheel of St Katherine Gold.

Crest: A carbuncle of twelve rays Or and surmounting the boss a merchant's cap Sable.

Supporters: Dexter, a dolphin hauriant Argent finned eyed scaled and tusked Gules; sinister, a sea-dragon Argent eyed langued finned and scaled Gules. The compartment a quayside with two flights of steps proper rising from water barry wavy Azure Argent and Azure.

Granted: 17 August 1987.

Water Conservators

Arms: Azure between a Cross Argent thereon nine Goutts de larmes cotised also Argent between four Water Bougets Gold

Crest: Issuant from a Circlet of Borage Flowers proper a Wolf's Head Gold.

Supporters: Dexter: A Beaver Sinister: An Otter, each supporting by the exterior forepaw a Shovel Or and standing on a grassy compartment proper.

Granted: 8 June 1991.

Firefighters

Arms: Quarterly 1 and 3 Argent on 3 bars wavy Azure a firehelmet Or and 2 and 4 Argent over all a Cross Gules and in pale a sword wards downwards Argent.

Crest: On a mural crown charged with a cross Gules a Salamander reguardant Or with flames issuant from its mouth and body Gules

Supporters: Dexter An heraldic Sealion Or langued Gules holding an 18th Century fireman's axe Sable. Sinister: A Dragon Or langued Gules holding a 'squirt' Sable.

Granted: 20 September 1996.

Hackney Carriage Drivers

Arms: Vert, a carriage wheel between three spurs in pall rowels outwards Or.

Crest: Issuant from flames proper a double-headed phoenix Sable holding in each beak a spur rowels downwards Or.

Supporters: Dexter, a horse Or supporting with the interior hind foot a carriage wheel Sable; sinister, a horse Sable supporting with the interior hind foot a carriage wheel Or.

Granted: 10 January 2003.

Management Consultants

Arms: Argent a comet its four trails in bend wavy at the head a mullet of six points in dexter chief over all a sword erect blade upwards all Gules.

Crest: Issuant from a crest coronet composed of a rim Or set thereon roses Argent and Gules barbed and seeded proper (five manifest) a cubit arms vested Argent the hand proper holding a comet as in the arms Gold.

Supporters: Dexter, a dragon, and sinister, a winged lion both per fess Argent and Gules langued and armed Gules semy of mullets of five points counter-changed.

Granted: 1 September 1995.

International Bankers

Arms: Per pale Sable and Gules a dragon rampant Argent within an orle of ten bezants.

Crest: In front of a yacht composed of the hull of a caravel redunda Sable and a mast Or rigged as a Bermudan sloop sails Gules five bezants in fess.

Supporters: On either side a griffin Sable winged Gules beaked and holding in the exterior claws a pyx chest Or.

Granted: 26 July 2004.

Tax Advisers

Arms: Azure a saltire couped checky Or and Gules within a chain in orle Or.

Crest: An owl statant guardant Azure gorged with a collar engrailed compony Or and Gules holding in the dexter claws a money pouch Or.

Supporters: Dexter, a griffin Argent beaked and forelegged Or, sinister a Pegasus Argen maned and unguled Or, each gorged with a collar engrailed compony Or and Gules attached thereto a chain reflexed over the back and terminating in a ring Or. The compartment a grassy mount Vert growing therefrom thrift and London pride slipped and leaved proper.

Arms and crest granted 25 July 2000; supporters granted 10 December 2004.

Security Professionals

Arms: Party per fess indented acute Or and Azure three Portcullises chained counterchained.

Crest: Upon a Helm with a Wreath Or and Azure A Unicorn forcene Argent armed mained tufted and unguled Or the dexter forehoof enfiling the hasp of a Padlock Azure the sinister supporting a Terrestrial Globe Or the oceans Azure.

Supporters: Dexter: a Dragon Azure armed langued winged and gorged with a plain Collar attached thereto a chai reflexed over the back and holding in the sinister foreclaws a Key wards uppermost Or. Sinister: Griffin Azure beaked armed langued winged and holding in the dexter claws a Lightning Flash Or.

Granted: 27 August 2001.

SELECT BIBLIOGRAPHY

GENERAL

Armorial Bearings of the Guilds of London (1960)
British Numismatic Journal 1931-33
Ceremonial Barges on the River Thames (1997)
The City of London and its Livery Companies, 1944
City Livery Badges 1931-33
Coat Armour of Livery Companies (1914)
The Guilds of the City of London (1945)
Livery Companies of the City
The Story of the City Companies (c.1935)
Use of Metal (2008)

LIVERY COMPANIES

The Actuaries' Company (1979-2004) (2004)
Guild of Air Pilots & Air Navigators 1929-1964 (1967)
History of the Society of Apothecaries (1998)
Society of Apothecaries (1980)
The Company of Barbers & Surgeons (2000)
Armourers & Brasiers Company History (1930)
Men of Metal (2008) [Armourers & Brasiers]
Barbers and Barber-Surgeons of London (1979)
Notable Barber Surgeons (2008)
Basketmakers' Company History (1978)
History of the Worshipful Company of Basketmakers (revised 1978)
Records of the Basketmakers Company (1911 revised 1967)
The Worshipful Company of Blacksmiths (2010)
The Brewer's Company – A Short History (1977)
Plain Dealing Fellows (1986) [Broderers]
A Cut Above the Rest (2005) [Butchers]
The Butchers of London [1976]
Carpenters' Company History (1995)
The Worshipful Company of Carmen of London (revised edition 1961)
Carr and Carmen (1999)
Children of Stories: The Paviors Company (1999)
History of the Worshipful Company of Coachmakers (1977)
The Coachmakers' Company: A Second History (1966)
The Cooks' Company: A Second History (1966)

Cordwainers' Company History (1931)

The Curriers' Company – A Modern History (1968)

Handbook of the Collections. Part 1 Worshipful Company of Cutlers

Distillers' Company History (1996)

Dyers' Company History (1965)

A Well Engineered Company (2008) [Engineers]

Fanmakers' Company History (1977)

Fans and Fan Makers (2000)

Fletchers' Company History (1968)

History of the Founders' Company (1925)

Worshipful Company of Fuellers (2010)

Furniture Makers' Company History (1964)

Gardeners' Company History (1964)

The Girdlers' Company History (2004)

Glass Sellers Company History (1940)

History of the Company of Glaziers and Painters of Glass (2000)

Glaziers' Company History (1918)

Glovers' Company History (1982)

Gold & Silver Wyre Drawers Company (1979)

The Gunmakers' Company – A History (2008)

Haberdashers' Company History (1971)

A History of the Worshipful Company of Innholders (2002)

Ironmongers' Company History (1991)

The Worshipful Company of Joiners & Ceilers (1971)

Leathersellers' Company History (1994)

The Company of Makers of Playing Cards History (2001)

Master Mariners' Company History (1974)

History of the Merchant Taylors' Company (2004)

Musicians' Company History (1971)

The Needlemakers' Company History 1656 – 2006 (2006)

Painter-Stainers' Company History (1950)

Parish Clerks' Company History (1971)

Pattenmakers' Company History (1974)

Plaisterers Company History (1985)

History of the Worshipful Company of Plumbers (2000)

Poulters Company History (1965)

The History of the Guild of Saddlers (1956 revised)

Salters Company History (1994)

Scientific Instrument Makers' Company History (1977)

A Short Account of the Worshipful Company of Stationers (1903)

Seven Centuries of Light: The Tallow Chandlers Company (1999)

Watermen's Company History, Volume 5 (2008)

Weavers Company History (1972)

Wheelwrights Company History (1970)